WHAT YOUR COLLEAGUES ARE SAY[...]

This companion guide masterfully and succinctly offers leaders a crash course in the *why, what,* and *how* for effective implementation of PLC+ teams. With authentic examples, ready-to-use templates, and thought-provoking reflection exercises, this guide thoroughly equips leaders with planning and monitoring pieces that are often so elusive when attempting to launch (and sustain) an impactful PLC culture. I just wish it had been on the market a decade ago!

—**Tara Howard,** Dean of Instruction, Owensboro High School

As schools recover from pandemic achievement losses, educators need new teaching strategies specific to these fragile learners. Professional learning communities provide a supportive approach to instructional development as we strive to bring students back to grade level and beyond. *PLC+: A Playbook for Instructional Leaders* is a succinct guide for leaders to successfully implement pedagogy growth strategies with their teachers.

—**Stephanie A. Blake,** Science Department Head, OTC Middle College Alternative High School

PLC+: A Playbook for Instructional Leaders is the right book at the right time. Where many of our original PLC leaders are reaching retirement age, we're finding it necessary to revisit the core principles of PLCs, inspiring one another as we navigate turbulent times and leaning into the power of the PLC team. PLCs that use their time wisely advance student learning. Working together at optimal levels shows an advanced positive impact on overall school improvement. The fifteen major ideas provide resources in the form of self-assessments and tools to incorporate throughout a school year. I'd recommend *PLC+: A Playbook for Instructional Leaders* as an exceptional team book study as you approach your next school year.

—**Jill Gildea,** Superintendent of Schools, Park City School District

A successful school provides opportunities for teachers to collaborate on teaching and learning. *PLC+: A Playbook for Instructional Leaders* provides the know-how in not only acknowledging teacher voice but also the steps to a thriving school culture.

—**Elizabeth Alvarez,** Superintendent, Forest Park D91

Designing and implementing a professional learning community can be a complex and challenging process. This book is a beneficial resource and provides additional strategies and ideas to help instructional leaders create a more cohesive and productive team that ultimately leads to student success. This is a practical guide that includes various ideas and tools for leaders who want to enhance their leadership skills and abilities in the context of professional learning communities while leveraging others' strengths and skills, knowledge, and ideas. Overall, this is a valuable addition to any leader's toolkit, helping them to create the conditions for more effective and impactful PLCs.

—**Kelly Jensen,** Director, Curriculum and Instruction, Elementary

PLC+

PLC+

A PLAYBOOK FOR
INSTRUCTIONAL
LEADERS

A COMPANION TO
THE PLC+
PLAYBOOK

NANCY FREY · DAVE NAGEL · DOUGLAS FISHER

TONI FADDIS · AIDA ALLEN-ROTELL

CORWIN

FOR INFORMATION:

Corwin

A SAGE Company

2455 Teller Road

Thousand Oaks, California 91320

(800) 233-9936

www.corwin.com

SAGE Publications Ltd.

1 Oliver's Yard

55 City Road

London EC1Y 1SP

United Kingdom

SAGE Publications India Pvt. Ltd.

Unit No 323-333, Third Floor, F-Block

International Trade Tower Nehru Place

New Delhi 110 019

India

SAGE Publications Asia-Pacific Pte. Ltd.

18 Cross Street #10-10/11/12

China Square Central

Singapore 048423

Vice President and
  Editorial Director: Monica Eckman

Director and Publisher,
  Corwin Classroom: Lisa Luedeke

Associate Content
  Development Editor: Sarah Ross

Production Editor: Melanie Birdsall

Typesetter: C&M Digitals (P) Ltd.

Proofreader: Theresa Kay

Indexer: Sheila Hill

Cover Designer: Gail Buschman

Marketing Manager: Megan Naidl

Printed in the United States of America

ISBN 9781071921487

Library of Congress Control Number: 2023939271

This book is printed on acid-free paper.

23 24 25 26 27 10 9 8 7 6 5 4 3 2 1

CONTENTS

About the Authors   xi

Acknowledgments   xv

INTRODUCTION   1

IDEA 1: NOT EVERYTHING WORKS, AND WE CAN LEARN FROM WHAT DOES NOT WORK IN PROFESSIONAL LEARNING COMMUNITIES.   9

IDEA 2: THE NEXT GENERATION OF PROFESSIONAL LEARNING COMMUNITIES MUST ADDRESS THE BARRIERS THAT HAVE CONFRONTED CURRENT PLC EFFORTS.   15

IDEA 3: QUALITY QUESTIONS DRIVE THE DISCUSSIONS AND DECISIONS THAT TEAMS MAKE AS PART OF THE PLC+ PROCESS.   27

IDEA 4: THERE ARE SPECIFIC ENABLING CONDITIONS THAT ALLOW PROFESSIONAL LEARNING COMMUNITIES TO THRIVE.   39

IDEA 5: HAVING A TIGHT-LOOSE-TIGHT MODEL ALLOWS FOR PURPOSE, AUTONOMY, AND MASTERY IN COLLABORATIVE MODELS OF TEACHER TEAMS.   47

IDEA 6: TEAMS NEED A GOAL, WHICH WE CALL
THE *COMMON CHALLENGE*, IN PLC+ WORK.   55

IDEA 7: PROFESSIONAL LEARNING OPPORTUNITIES
SHOULD BE ALIGNED WITH, AND COMPLEMENTARY
TO, THE WORK TEACHERS ARE DOING IN THEIR
PROFESSIONAL LEARNING COMMUNITIES.   65

IDEA 8: THERE IS A STRONG RELATIONSHIP
BETWEEN TEACHER CREDIBILITY AND
COLLECTIVE TEACHER EFFICACY (AND BOTH
ARE IMPORTANT FOR PLCS TO FUNCTION WELL).   77

IDEA 9: THERE'S MORE THAN ONE WAY
TO FORM PLC+ TEAMS.   87

IDEA 10: LEADERS NEED TO IDENTIFY TRENDS
AND DEVELOP PLANS TO SUPPORT EDUCATORS
AS THEY WORK TOGETHER.   97

IDEA 11: ACTIVATORS ARE CRUCIAL TO
HELPING ENSURE THE LEARNING OF ALL
ADULTS IN PLC+ SETTINGS.   111

IDEA 12: TEACHERS NEW TO THE PROFESSION
OR NEW TO THE SCHOOL REQUIRE ATTENTION
FOR THE PROFESSIONAL LEARNING
COMMUNITY TO THRIVE.   121

IDEA 13: LEADERS CAN ASSIST PLC+
TEAMS IN DETERMINING THEIR IMPACT.   131

IDEA 14: LEADERS SPREAD INNOVATIONS
ACROSS THE SCHOOLWIDE PLC+.   139

IDEA 15: LEADERS NEED TO COMMUNICATE IMPACT
TO STAKEHOLDERS BEYOND THE PROFESSIONAL
LEARNING COMMUNITY.   153

Coda   **165**

References   **167**

Index   **171**

Visit the companion website at
resources.corwin.com/PLC+forleaders
for downloadable resources.

ABOUT THE AUTHORS

Nancy Frey is a professor in educational leadership at San Diego State University and a teacher leader at Health Sciences High and Middle College. She is a member of the International Literacy Association's Literacy Research Panel. Her published titles include *Visible Learning for Literacy, This Is Balanced Literacy, Removing Labels, Rebound, The Social-Emotional Learning Playbook,* and *How Scaffolding Works*. Nancy is a credentialed special educator, reading specialist, and administrator in California and learns from teachers and students every day.

Dave Nagel began his educational career as a middle school science and high school biology teacher. His administrative experiences involved positions as a middle school assistant principal, high school associate principal, and director of extended day and credit recovery programs. He was honored numerous times as a Senior Choice winner, where graduating seniors selected him as someone who dramatically affected their lives in a positive way. He has worked extensively in leading effective collaborative efforts with schools and districts across the country. He is passionate about supporting school leaders to establish conditions where teacher learning and collective efficacy can thrive. Dave is the author of *Effective Grading Practices for Secondary Teachers* and the co-author of the PLC+ series of publications.

Douglas Fisher is a professor and chair of educational leadership at San Diego State University and a teacher leader at Health Sciences High and Middle College. Previously, Doug was an early intervention teacher and elementary school educator. He is the recipient of an International Reading Association William S. Grey citation of merit and an Exemplary Leader award from the Conference on English Leadership of the National Council of Teachers of English (NCTE), as well as a Christa McAuliffe award for excellence in teacher education. In 2022, he was inducted into the Reading Hall of Fame by the Literacy Research Association. He has published numerous articles on reading and literacy, differentiated instruction, and curriculum design, as well as books such as *The Teacher Clarity Playbook, PLC+, Visible Learning for Literacy, Comprehension: The Skill, Will, and Thrill of Reading, How Feedback Works, Teaching Reading,* and, most recently, *Teaching Students to Drive Their Learning.*

Toni Faddis was a bilingual teacher in an elementary school as well as a principal in San Diego. In addition, Toni served as a district central office leader, responsible for equity, access, and leadership development. She holds teaching and administrative services credentials in California and earned her doctoral degree in educational leadership from San Diego State University. Toni also mentors and coaches current and aspiring school leaders in the educational leadership department at San Diego State University. Toni is the co-author of *Collaborating Through Collective Efficacy Cycles: Ensuring All Students and Teachers Succeed* and *The Ethical Line.*

Aida Allen-Rotell was a bilingual teacher in an elementary school where she taught grades K–6 for 15 years, as well as a high school special educator, academic coach, coordinator of services for multilingual learners, and administrator. She holds teaching and administrative services credentials in California and earned her master's degree in education from San Diego State University. She led efforts to improve student learning that resulted in her school earning academic distinction for impacting the lives of students living in poverty, becoming a Visible Learning Gold Certified school, and improving academic language for multilingual learners. She also served as an adviser to many high school clubs, was the student government adviser, and led students to championships for ten years in Health Occupations Students Association (HOSA) competitions. She is dedicated to developing teacher and leadership mindsets for diverse learning populations.

ACKNOWLEDGMENTS

Corwin gratefully acknowledges the contributions of the following reviewers:

Elizabeth Alvarez
Superintendent, Forest Park D91
Chicago, IL

Stephanie Blake
Science Department Head, OTC Middle College Alternative High School
Springfield, MO

Jill Gildea
Superintendent of Schools, Park City School District
Park City, UT

Tara Howard
Dean of Instruction, Owensboro High School
Owensboro, KY

Renee Peoples
Instructional Coach, Swain County Schools
Whittier, NC

INTRODUCTION

How can instructional leaders inspire educators to be their collective best selves—especially if the teachers need more support to comfortably work as a team? Some teams are friendly with each other, communicate well together, and do a good job without much outside direction. Other teams, however, have habits that are concerning—ranging from social loafing to drama to insubordination. These negative scenarios are commonplace in schools, and instructional leaders often struggle to find the balance of nudging teams forward without shutting them down altogether. To make matters even more challenging, instructional leaders don't always receive training in how to effectively structure and successfully orchestrate multiple professional learning community teams on a campus. Instead, instructional leaders are often told, "You've got this" and "You'll figure it out," which may cause them to feel isolated and alone, wondering how to succeed among so many competing interests and needs.

THE INSTRUCTIONAL LEADER'S ROLE IN PLC+

It's likely that you became an instructional leader because you were an outstanding teacher. While in the classroom, you honed your craft and figured out how to leverage student motivation so that learners could achieve at high levels. The culture in your classroom was likely positive, students were excited to learn, and you looked forward to going to work every morning. Fast forward a few years: now you're the instructional leader, and you find that your inner critic has a lot to say to you—filling your head with doubts and possibly shaking your confidence. This is challenging because you're the instructional leader, after all—you're expected to know how to lead others.

The skills and dispositions that make someone a great teacher don't immediately translate to situations where your main job is to motivate adults. And evidence of your leadership skills is often interpreted through the lens of publicly reported student achievement data. Your track record as an individual teacher is mostly forgotten now. Your responsibilities have expanded, so you are now responsible for ensuring every student in your school receives a top-notch educational experience, not just the thirty-three students in your former classroom.

This is the challenge of contemporary school leadership: organizing individual teachers into a cohesive professional learning community they all want to be part of because the spotlight is on focus, drive, and a relentless pursuit of excellence for all students. It is important to note that there is only one professional learning community: the school. Teacher teams operate within this single community to learn from one another and to spread innovation across teams. This is at the heart of a PLC+ approach: *Teacher teams investigate and innovate in order to develop sustainable, long-term solutions for the entire organization.* But in order to do so, the professional learning community—the school—must develop the professional capital to do so. And here's where you come in.

WHAT MATTERS IN THE PROFESSIONAL CAPITAL OF SCHOOLS?

Research over the last few decades has revealed much about the value of effective instructional leaders in relation to student learning and educators' professional satisfaction. Building the cohesion of a school's efforts requires investing in the professional capital of the group (Hargreaves & Fullan, 2012). Think of *capital* as the reserves an organization can draw upon. Some school organizations are richer in terms of their professional capital, while others do not have the same amount of "wealth" to apply when facing challenges.

Professional capital refers to the mix of social, human, and decisional capital possessed by the adults in an organization. Professional capital is the sum of three dimensions. The first is *social capital,* a measure of the quality of the trusting relationships among those adults, while the second is *human capital*, a measure of the professional skills of the organization's members. Hargreaves and Fullan examined the work of Leana (2011), an organizational management researcher who studied the effects that the human and social capital of multiple schools' adults had on student learning. To gauge impact, she measured each element in 130 schools and correlated them to mathematics achievement at the beginning and end of the school year. Schools with high social capital among the adults (trusting, collaborative relationships) did well. Schools with both high social capital and human capital (technical skills) did even better.

Here's where it gets interesting. *Students whose teachers possessed low human capital (technical skills) did better if they attended a school with high social capital among the adults.* In other words, the network of relationships among the adults served as the lubricant for technical skills to emerge. When the conditions allow for staff to collaborate meaningfully with others, good teaching rubs off. You can build the technical skills of the staff (human capital) when the environment supports adult collaboration (social capital).

Decisional capital—a measure of the permission teachers have to make judgments and decisions—is the third factor Hargreaves and Fullan (2012) identified as a contributor to the overall professional capital of schools. Educators must not only possess the technical skills required for the classroom; they must also acquire an increasing ability over their careers to make decisions—both in the moment of active teaching (a practice referred to as *noticing*) and in planning future instruction. The ability to reflect, make decisions, and collaborate with

This is the challenge of contemporary school leadership: organizing individual teachers into a cohesive professional learning community they all want to be part of because the spotlight is on focus, drive, and a relentless pursuit of excellence for all students.

others are all necessary for decisional capital to grow. Similarly, organizations can build human capital through decisional capital. The PLC+ framework allows for all three elements—social, human, and decisional capital—to grow.

WHAT MATTERS IN INSTRUCTIONAL LEADERSHIP?

Instructional leadership harnesses the professional capital of the school organization. Robinson's (2011) work on instructional leadership is especially enlightening, noting that there are five dimensions at play, each with its own effect size—the overall magnitude of an influence on student learning.

1. Leading teacher learning and development (effect size = 0.84)

2. Establishing goals and expectations (effect size = 0.42)

3. Ensuring quality teaching (effect size = 0.42)

4. Resourcing strategically (effect size = 0.31)

5. Ensuring a safe and orderly learning environment (effect size = 0.27)

She calls this "student-centered leadership" for a reason: leading teacher learning and development holds a strong potential for impacting student learning. To be clear, other dimensions, such as locating resources and assuring a safe and orderly environment, are also important. Further, the more that each of these five conditions is evidenced, the more likely it is that leaders will have a positive impact on student learning (Robinson, 2011).

VISIBLE LEARNING

This book draws on the vast Visible Learning® research collection (Visible Learning Meta^X, 2021; www.visiblelearningmetax.com). For those unfamiliar with Visible Learning research, consider that John Hattie has been collecting meta-analyses for many years. At this point, there are more than 2,100 of them, representing 350,000,000 learners worldwide (Hattie, 2023). Meta-analyses are collections of studies, sometimes hundreds of them, that allow researchers to determine effect size. Hattie has identified 350 influences on learning, and the average effect size of all of them combined is 0.40. As an example, boredom has an effect size of −0.47 on student learning, which means it has a significant potential to negatively influence performance.

In contrast, influences that fall above an effect size of 0.40 possess an increasingly strong potential to accelerate student learning. For instance, collective teacher efficacy, a major feature and desired outcome of professional learning communities, has an effect size of 1.39. This means a group of teachers who understand they have the wherewithal to impact student learning are quite likely to do so.

> The PLC+ framework allows for all three elements—social, human, and decisional capital—to grow.

Now consider again the effect sizes Robinson (2011) reported on dimensions of instructional leadership: leading teacher learning and development (effect size = 0.84); establishing goals and expectations (effect size = 0.42); ensuring quality teaching (effect size = 0.42); resourcing strategically (effect size = 0.31); and ensuring a safe and orderly learning environment (effect size = 0.27). Clearly, your attention to leading and managing PLC+ teams is well-placed.

We have used the Visible Learning database to make some of the recommendations in this book. For others, we have drawn on the experiences of leaders who have evidence of their impact on the professional learning communities they lead.

PURPOSE OF THIS COMPANION PLAYBOOK

We have envisioned this companion playbook as a tool to equip you with the latest evidence on teaching, learning, and leading in concise and useful ways. We aim to provide you with strategies and techniques that foster and promote cohesive teams and the collaborative learning of adults on your campus. We strive to help you to further individual teacher credibility, which is vital in classrooms, and foster the conditions for collective teacher efficacy to emerge across your campus.

Effective instructional leaders recognize the value of PLC+ teams and other teams of educators working together. Meta-analyses and systematic reviews of the research confirm the benefits of teacher collaboration: increased student learning and well-being outcomes, greater teacher satisfaction rates, and increased capacities to onboard new teachers or new members to the team (Baker-Doyle, 2012; García-Martínez et al., 2021; Vangrieken et al., 2015).

We focus primarily on instructional leadership in this companion playbook because of the known positive impact it has on student learning. That said, we recognize that site-level programs may be disconnected or fragmented without the instructional leader's attention to school operations. The focus, therefore, is on supporting PLC+ teams to function at high levels.

ORGANIZATION OF THE PLAYBOOK

Throughout this companion playbook, you'll find that we refer to teacher teams and PLC+ teams interchangeably. In addition, we ground this work on the core principles of a PLC+ framework, with five guiding questions that inform every investigation cycle, and four cross-cutting values that are infused within each of the guiding questions (see Figure i.1). The questions and cross-cutting values are also the focus of Idea 2 and Idea 3 in this companion playbook. You'll find more detailed information about how these questions and values are operationalized in the anchor book of this series, *PLC+: Better Decisions and Greater Impact by Design* (Fisher et al., 2019a), and in other related PLC+ publications. This companion playbook is designed with the instructional leader in mind. Here we offer specific instructional leadership actions and behaviors that promote cohesion and professional learning in a PLC+ organization.

FIGURE i.1

THE PLC+ FRAMEWORK

PLC+ GUIDING QUESTIONS	PLC+ CROSS-CUTTING VALUES
1. Where are we going?	High Expectations
2. Where are we now?	Activation
3. How do we move learning forward?	Individual and Collective Teacher Efficacy
4. What did we learn today?	Equity
5. Who benefited and who did not benefit?	

Source: Fisher et al. (2019b).

Effective instructional leaders recognize the value of PLC+ teams and other teams of educators working together.

We have organized this companion playbook according to fifteen major ideas and an accompanying essential question. This companion playbook provides many tools you can use tomorrow and throughout the school year. There are spaces to record your observations and reflections (Pause and Ponder), as well as a self-assessment of the school aligned to each major idea.

NOTES

_____

_____

_____

_____

_____

_____

_____

_____

_____

_____

_____

_____

	KEY IDEAS	ESSENTIAL QUESTIONS
Idea 1	Not everything works, and we can learn from what does not work in professional learning communities.	*How can we use lessons learned from previous attempts at implementing professional learning communities to improve the quality of the teams in our school or district?*
Idea 2	The next generation of professional learning communities must address the barriers that have confronted current PLC efforts.	*What must change to improve the experiences teachers have with their colleagues as they collaborate?*
Idea 3	Quality questions drive the discussions and decisions that teams make as part of the PLC+ process.	*What discussion drivers are necessary for teams to assume collective responsibility for students' learning and support each other in continuous improvement?*
Idea 4	There are specific enabling conditions that allow professional learning communities to thrive.	*What conditions are present in the teams at our school, and how can I identify leadership actions that promote effective and efficient teams?*
Idea 5	Having a tight-loose-tight model allows for purpose, autonomy, and mastery in collaborative models of teacher teams.	*How are you currently providing clarity of expectations as well as opportunities for both ownership and accountability in PLC+ teams?*
Idea 6	Teams need a goal, which we call the *common challenge,* in PLC+ work.	*What are the challenges that teachers face when it comes to student learning, and how might they collaborate to address those challenges?*
Idea 7	Professional learning opportunities should be aligned with, and complementary to, the work teachers are doing in their professional learning communities.	*How can the school's or district's professional learning calendar of offerings consider teachers' desired learning?*
Idea 8	There is a strong relationship between teacher credibility and collective teacher efficacy (and both are important for PLCs to function well).	*What is my role as a leader in developing teacher credibility and fostering collective teacher efficacy?*
Idea 9	There's more than one way to form PLC+ teams.	*How should teacher teams be formed to ensure that adult learning is facilitated such that student learning is enhanced?*
Idea 10	Leaders need to identify trends and develop plans to support educators as they work together.	*What patterns am I noticing in different teams, and what actions should the leadership team and I take to support teacher learning?*
Idea 11	Activators are crucial to helping ensure the learning of all adults in PLC+ settings.	*How are you currently supporting and developing activators as drivers of learning within your PLC+ structure?*
Idea 12	Teachers new to the profession or new to the school require attention for the professional learning community to thrive.	*How do we ensure that new teachers feel welcomed into the school and are acclimated to how adults learn together?*
Idea 13	Leaders can assist PLC+ teams in determining their impact.	*What structures are in place in your school so that PLC+ teams understand their impact?*
Idea 14	Leaders spread innovations across the schoolwide PLC+.	*What are some ways to spread effective teaching and learning strategies across the schoolwide professional learning community?*
Idea 15	Leaders need to communicate impact to stakeholders beyond the professional learning community.	*How do you ensure that external stakeholders—including families, other schools, district leaders, and the superintendent—know about innovations at your school?*

Each major idea begins with background information designed to boost your knowledge about effectively working with adults. The intention is to provide you with the most essential information needed to lead PLC+ teams—and to gradually release these teams to be interdependent, productive collaborators who use their time wisely and advance student learning. To do so, we provide leadership tools to support your ability to inspire others to work together at optimal levels. These range from independent reflections to activities that you can implement with teams or with your whole staff. We hope you'll feel more equipped to lead and increase learning-centered conversations with individual teachers, with teacher teams, and with the larger learning community.

We offer examples and non-examples throughout to provide some insight into our leadership thinking: how we organized our time, the decisions we made, what went well, what bombed, and what we learned from each situation. From experience, we know that being proactive and determining how we'll spend our time is more empowering and joyful than allowing the daily fires to take over. We are reminded of a quote that's often misattributed to Ralph Waldo Emerson, but solid advice nonetheless: "Don't be pushed by your problems. Be led by your dreams."

NOTES

NOTES

Idea 1

NOT EVERYTHING WORKS, AND WE CAN LEARN FROM WHAT DOES NOT WORK IN PROFESSIONAL LEARNING COMMUNITIES.

Essential Question: How can we use lessons learned from previous attempts at implementing professional learning communities to improve the quality of the teams in our school or district?

The concept of professional learning communities (PLCs) has existed in education for many decades. The phrase *professional learning community* entered the educational lexicon in the 1990s after Senge's (1990) book *The Fifth Discipline* was published. Myers and Myers used the phrase *professional learning community* in their 1995 book. Myers presented the first paper on PLCs at the American Association for Educational Research in 1996. In 1997, Hord published a white paper titled "Professional Learning Communities: Communities of Continuous Inquiry and Improvement." You can see Shirley Hord talk about the origins of this idea at https://youtu.be/ZgKrNkeiF-w (Masood, 2021). A year later, in 1998, DuFour and Eaker (1998) published their book, *Professional Learning Communities at Work*. The rest is history. PLCs have become a common feature in schools around the world.

Unfortunately, PLCs often fail to deliver on their promise (e.g., Sims & Penny, 2015), despite the evidence that they can be an effective way to improve student learning (e.g., Vescio et al., 2008). To help leaders avoid the mistakes made in the past and to ensure they don't unintentionally contribute to the cynicism that exists about PLCs being "just another meeting" (Fisher et al., 2009), let's examine why this good idea often fails to make a difference.

1. SMART goals are not necessary for PLC success.

One mistake that leaders make is requiring teams to *always* develop a SMART (specific, measurable, achievable, relevant, and time-bound) goal. Far too often, this takes valuable time away from the conversations that teams of teachers can and should have about evidence of student learning. It can take weeks to identify and agree on a SMART goal. In some cases, leaders choose and assign the SMART goal, applying it to all teams within the school.

Yes, we need to improve student learning, and analyzing data is important. But teams work on issues that are currently challenging them, and they want the freedom to revise their focus throughout the year as they learn about their students' strengths and needs. Annual SMART goals can thwart the learning of teams, especially when the teams view the SMART goals as a compliance activity that they complete only because it's a rule. We will focus on *common challenges*, which is the term we use for the goals a team sets for itself, later in this companion guide.

PAUSE AND PONDER

How does your school, district, or organization currently use SMART goals? Is this effective? How might freeing people from this task help them focus on student learning?

2. Course-alike teams are only one way to structure learning communities.

Conventionally, teams have essentially been "marriages of convenience," with teachers forced to be part of a specific team based on what they teach. The logic for this was that teachers only could talk with colleagues who taught the same thing as they did, which would allow people to share and examine data about the same learning expectations.

There are so many problems with this. For example, in many secondary schools, teachers teach more than one class, such as World History and U.S. History, or seventh- and eighth-grade English. Which meeting should they attend? And what happens to the discussions about learning in the classes for which the teacher does not attend team meetings? Also, what should leaders do with the singletons: the lone elementary PE teacher or art teacher? Or the high school teacher who is the only one who teaches calculus or chemistry? And what about all the specialists: counselors, speech and language specialists, behavior specialists, and so on? What should they do? Further, this structure fails to capitalize on the power of vertical alignment and the conversations that teachers can have across grade levels or across departments. We'll focus on forming teams later in this companion guide.

PAUSE AND PONDER

Currently, how are PLC+ teams configured at your site? How do singletons collaborate with other educators? How often and how effective are these arrangements? What ideas do you have for future configurations to enhance PLC+ teams' impact?

3. Response to Intervention (RTI)/Multi-Tiered Systems of Support (MTSS) cannot be the default solution when students do not respond to the instruction.

From our perspective, PLC and RTI/MTSS are too closely aligned. Yes, some students need interventions. However, the percentage of students who are sent to intervention continues to increase, and the risk is that teacher teams abdicate their responsibility for those students. Note that we said "sent to intervention" rather than "receive intervention." In too many places, RTI/MTSS and special education are places where students are sent to—to other teachers, assistants, or specialists—and thus the general education teachers no longer have responsibility for their learning.

> The whole point of a school's learning community is to develop collective responsibility for students' learning.

The whole point of a school's learning community is to develop collective responsibility for students' learning. The team is responsible for *all* of the students they serve. The team can access interventions as needed to meet students' needs, but it is the team that remains responsible. Services should not override responsibility for students.

Further, when RTI/MTSS and PLC are too closely linked, teachers do not focus on providing necessary opportunities for student learning or on removing barriers to student learning because the model suggests that when students don't learn, the only answer is intervention somewhere else. We'll focus on barrier removal and opportunities to learn later in this companion guide.

PAUSE AND PONDER

At your school, is RTI/MTSS used as a fix-it strategy to defer responsibility for students who aren't making the expected progress? How might teams coordinate, time, and share the responsibility to collaborate with other teams (such as MTSS, Special Education, Student Success Team, and others) in order to accelerate student learning?

4. Common formative assessments are not the only way to talk about evidence.

Teacher teams should talk about evidence of student learning. Teams, and individual members of those teams, need to determine the impact their efforts are having on students. But common formative assessments force teachers to collaborate only with people who teach exactly the same thing they do, which we have already discussed as problematic. In addition, the development of common formative assessments takes time, and not all of us are skilled at assessment construction. That time is probably better spent focused on what we can do with the evidence, rather than on debating items on the common assessment.

To combat this, some districts develop common formative assessments for teachers to use. In this case, teachers can become cynical; some may even teach the test rather than the content so their students appear stronger than they are. Again, we believe that teacher teams should discuss evidence, and we recognize that there are a lot of different sources of evidence that can inform teacher practice. However, research indicates that the vast majority of conversations in data teams are focused on explaining away the data rather than discussing what actions can be taken to address the realities of the data. In fact, Evans et al. (2019) found that 85% of the minutes in data team discussions were focused on dismissing the data, with the majority of comments falling into four categories:

- Student behavior (e.g., "not paying attention")
- A mismatch between the assessment demands and the student (e.g., "he's an English language learner")
- Students' home life (e.g., "they don't read at home")
- Suspected or established underlying conditions (e.g., "I think she's dyslexic")

Thus, only 15% of the time was devoted to actions that teachers and teams could take to ensure student learning. We'll focus on data discussions later in this companion guide.

PAUSE AND PONDER

How and when do the PLC+ teams at your site discuss student learning? What types of evidence do teams currently collect? What ideas do you have to keep conversations focused on what teachers have control of?

SELF-ASSESSMENT

Use the circles below to analyze the teams in your school or district. What is in your sphere of influence or control, and what is in your sphere of concern? Throughout this guidebook, we'll ask you to work on aspects that are within your sphere of influence.

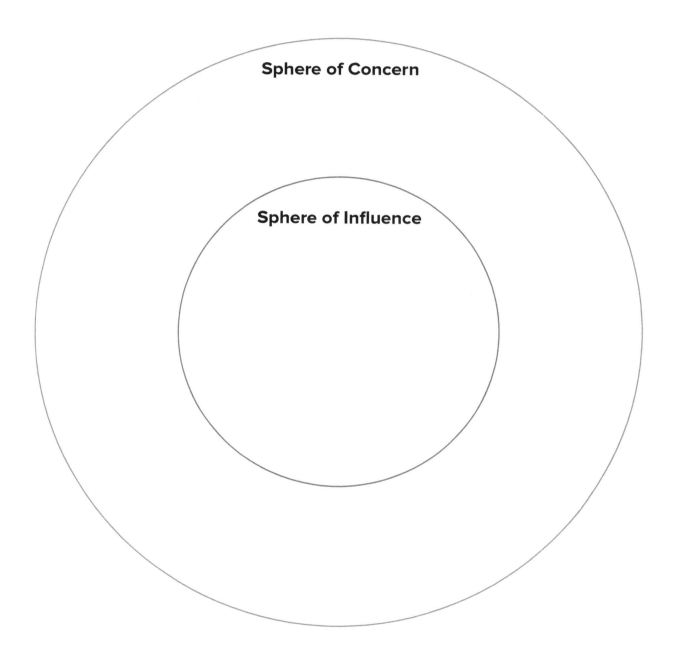

Sphere of Concern

Sphere of Influence

Visit the companion website at
resources.corwin.com/PLC+forleaders
for downloadable resources.

Idea 2

THE NEXT GENERATION OF PROFESSIONAL LEARNING COMMUNITIES MUST ADDRESS THE BARRIERS THAT HAVE CONFRONTED CURRENT PLC EFFORTS.

Essential Question: What must change to improve the experiences teachers have with their colleagues as they collaborate?

Since their inception, professional learning communities have been positioned as an important catalyst for school improvement from within the organization. However, from the beginning, Hord (1980) cautioned that a fundamental mis-understanding of the ways adults work together could undermine these efforts. The problem? Groups that function cooperatively—but not collaboratively. Hord noted that while collaborative groups operated using shared agreements about focus, tasks, and results, cooperative groups placed a higher value on helping each other. In the cooperative model, results tend to be more variable and less predictable. She notes that in a cooperative model, there is mutual agreement, but they do not progress beyond that point. A group may agree on a topic for their learning community work, but not move further than the study of the topic. A collaborative group, on the other hand, not only arrives at an agreement about the topic but also implements and executes a plan for improvement. Or to use another analogy: "Dating is a cooperative venture, while marriage is a collaborative one" (Hord, 1980, p. 6).

What is the current status of PLC teams at your school? Do they operate as cooperative models or collaborative models? What is your evidence? Regarding the current status, what do you see as benefits and barriers to their work?

DECAY

Decay is a further issue when it comes to how groups work together. The extensive content responsibilities of teacher preparation programs leave little room for learning about how adults work with others. This omission has negative consequences when a teacher who is new to the profession is hired at a school and learns only that "PLC meetings are on Wednesday afternoons." For teachers who lack basic background information about best practices for PLC meetings, the PLC processes become whatever the existing hyper-local traditions are. Over time, the processes and purposes of the professional learning community decay, and what gets perpetuated is a mere shadow of what they were originally designed to accomplish.

Ever play the telephone game, where a sentence is whispered into the ear of the first person in line, and then subsequently passed through a series of whispers to the rest? The end result is hilariously different than the original message. In the case of professional learning communities, however, the decay is not so funny. It's little wonder that during these meetings, many teams end up either planning next week's lessons (not always together) or talking about next week's field trip. They are working cooperatively, but not collaboratively. Don't mistake activity for results.

PAUSE AND PONDER

When was the last time the faculty had formal training in the purpose and operations of professional learning communities? Now compare this to the initial employment dates of teachers at your school. What percentage of teachers at your school have not had training? Why might this be a hindrance to your work?

THE NEXT GENERATION: PLC+

Schooling in the third decade of this century is vastly different than schooling in the 1990s. And yet in some cases, school organizations might be continuing to cling to models developed decades ago that don't reflect contemporary issues in schooling. The design of the PLC+ framework, noted in Figure 2.1, outlines the five guiding questions and four cross-cutting values, which are meant to reflect changing conditions.

FIGURE 2.1

THE PLC+ FRAMEWORK

PLC+ GUIDING QUESTIONS	PLC+ CROSS-CUTTING VALUES
1. Where are we going?	Equity
2. Where are we now?	High Expectations
3. How do we move learning forward?	Individual and Collective Efficacy
4. What did we learn today?	Activation
5. Who benefited and who did not benefit?	

Source: Fisher et al. (2019b).

While the guiding questions drive the investigation cycle, the cross-cutting values are manifested within each of the questions:

- **Equity.** Information is processed to identify and apply appropriate and impactful evidence-based instructional practices and culturally responsive teaching that values the background of every student and helps prepare each of them for success. Valuing the assets each learner brings to the classroom requires ensuring instruction, curriculum, and assessment are responsive and affirming.

- **High expectations.** PLC+ teams manifest high-expectations teaching by ensuring that grade-level and course standards are taught. This requires not only holding all students accountable for reaching mastery but also holding ourselves accountable for teaching with high expectations.

- **Individual and collective efficacy.** There is an incredible amount of brain power we can capitalize on when we take our individual capacity and contribute it to a collective whole. This model asks us to use our collective efficacy to create the belief that we can make an impact on each and every one of our students and align our beliefs with actions to make it so.

- **Activation.** High-functioning PLC+ teams don't just happen by chance. They require deliberate efforts and structures put in place to ensure they are efficient and focused. This requires skilled facilitation as well as participation. The team relies on the growing ability of all its members to activate the thinking and action of others.

The next generation of professional learning communities begins with an understanding of what students already know. Instructional time is far too precious to be squandered teaching students things they already know. Yet the evidence is that approximately 40% of instructional time is spent on things students already know (Nuthall, 2007). The problem, of course, is that it isn't the same 40% across students—there is variability in what each learner already knows.

The second question in PLC+ focuses directly on this issue: *Where are we now?* This is consistent with the mounting data on teacher clarity as a formidable driver for learning. John Hattie's Visible Learning database reports that teaching with clarity holds an effect size of 0.85, representing a high potential for accelerating student learning (Visible Learning Meta^X, 2021; www.visiblelearningmetax.com). Knowing where students are now, in advance of new learning, sets the stage for understanding our impact.

The next generation of professional learning communities must engage educators in conversations about effective instruction. Knowing our starting point is important, but knowing how we can advance learning is crucial. We should never be left guessing about how to move students' learning forward. In the same way that doctors monitor the trajectory of their patients' treatment and recovery, educators must monitor how their students are progressing this week. We can't afford to wait until the end of the unit, semester, or course to learn about what's working and what's not. Imagine if a doctor's only monitoring tool was whether a patient lived or died. We would call that malpractice. Failing to monitor and respond to students' progress is educational malpractice.

The next generation of professional learning communities must ignite the knowledge of the team by activating dialogue on the most important topics. Adults who don't really know how to work together are at risk of falling into a pattern of cooperation rather than collaboration. The maintenance of the social contract is paramount; friendships rule the day. But a team that is friendly isn't automatically a team that is productive. So how do we reconcile these two—at times—competing values? We must ensure that teams are equipped with tools and processes they can use to activate each other's thinking in ways that are humane and growth producing. Rather than solely relying on an individual to parent the team, PLC+ situates the activation of team decision making and action in the hands of the team itself.

The next generation of professional learning communities must systematically deliver on the promise of equity. To date, no PLC framework has directly integrated equity into the discussions teachers have with each other. Yet no issue has driven schooling change in this century like equity.

Having said that, too often "equitable education" is hampered by a perception that it is at a distance from the classroom. But structural and institutional inequities are perpetuated through daily classroom practice. There is a saying that the last thing a fish notices is the water it swims in. The PLC+ framework seeks to make material the actions that teams take to disrupt barriers that are hiding in plain sight.

The next generation of professional learning communities must address students' opportunities to learn and remove barriers to learning. One barrier that is hiding in plain sight involves lowered expectations of teachers for their students, especially in the wake of COVID. Yet these lower expectations, manifested in teaching below grade level, existed before the pandemic; a 2022 report documented this trend in the years preceding the shutdown of in-person schooling (TNTP, 2022). This study of 150,000 classrooms examined the literacy experiences of students and reported these findings:

- Below-grade-level work increased by 5% in 2021–22 in the wake of the pandemic.

- Students in high-poverty schools spent 65% more time on below-grade-level literacy work than peers in more affluent schools.

- In classrooms where students of color dominate, 38% were *never* provided grade-level assignments, and only 44% of teachers believed their students could master the standards.

- Ironically, comparative success rates for the same student on grade-level and below-grade-level assignments revealed insignificant performance differences, equivalent to answering three additional questions correctly over the span of ten assignments.

The study's authors stated that "inequities in access to grade-level work that existed long before the pandemic have only deepened, and that most school systems are not yet implementing strategies that could put students on track to recover from the disruption of the last several years" (p. 2). A PLC+ framework seeks to correct these inequities of expectation through the systematic application of the first question, "Where are we going?" A return to what the standards actually say (not the folklore that emerges when teams fail to recalibrate) ensures that teaching for clarity is sufficiently challenging.

A new framework is needed if schools are to reflect the needs and assets that communities and students possess. Importantly, a new framework should amplify the educators who make up the professional learning community.

IDEAL STATE

Plato (1992) is attributed with the concept of an "ideal state," where those with different needs coexist and understand that groups are mutually dependent. Plato envisioned what this society would look like and how it would operate, but you don't need to be an ancient Greek philosopher to create a plan for what you hope to achieve for professional learning communities at your school or district. Begin by considering the questions in Figure 2.2.

FIGURE 2.2

WHAT IS YOUR IDEAL STATE?

What is your vision for professional learning communities 36 months from now?

What is your current state?

What success criteria will you use to measure progress toward goals?

SET EXPECTATIONS TO FRAME THE WORK AHEAD

Organizations use expectations to foster consistency and instill confidence in their staff. Unifying the staff to deliver on the school's core mission—student learning—can be a challenge if adults are not accustomed to collaborating (not just cooperating). Your expectations will evolve into the success criteria you will use to measure progress. Consider setting these success criteria using a timeline that sets interim goals along the way (see Figure 2.3).

FIGURE 2.3

SUCCESS CRITERIA TIMELINE

YEAR 1 SUCCESS CRITERIA FOR PLC+	YEAR 2 SUCCESS CRITERIA FOR PLC+	YEAR 3 SUCCESS CRITERIA FOR PLC+
Introduction: 30-day success criteria from the ideal state task (Monitoring and evaluation embedded)	Onboarding for new staff and Introduction of Year 1 revisions: 30-day success criteria (Monitoring and evaluation embedded)	Onboarding for new staff and Introduction of Year 2 revisions: 30-day success criteria (Monitoring and evaluation embedded)
Practice: 60-day success criteria (Monitoring and evaluation embedded)	Full Implementation: 90-day success criteria (Monitoring and evaluation embedded)	Full Implementation: 90-day success criteria (Monitoring and evaluation embedded)
Piloting: 90-day success criteria (Monitoring and evaluation embedded)	Continuous Improvement: 180-day success criteria (Monitoring and evaluation embedded for the purpose of revision)	Continuous Improvement: 180-day success criteria (Monitoring and evaluation embedded for the purpose of continued revision)
Refining: 180-day success criteria (Monitoring and evaluation embedded for the purpose of revision)		

The Institute for Organization Management, the professional development initiative of the U.S. Chamber of Commerce, says that setting expectations can be beneficial across six dimensions: *clarity, baseline for measurement, communication, empowerment, a reference point when expectations aren't met,* and *accountability to self and the school:*

- **Clarity.** When expectations are discussed and unpacked, you and the staff can get on the same page. Every rower knows that all the oars in the water need to be pulling in the same direction.

- **Baseline for measurement.** Instructional leadership requires communication, feedback, and goal setting. But when staff aren't clear on how their efforts contribute to the mission of the school, performance can suffer. Clear expectations equip staff with the calibration tools they need to guide their own performance.

- **Communication.** Stated expectations provide staff members with a common vocabulary of excellence.

- **Empowerment.** Expectations are not intended to be onerous, or to ensnare people in a game of "gotcha." Empowered staff are better able to make decisions that are consistent with guidelines. After all, you don't want everyone coming to you about every decision.

- **A reference point when expectations aren't met.** A staff member who struggles is a staff member in need of feedback. But feedback is much more difficult when the expectations haven't been clearly stated and enacted.

- **Accountability to self and the school.** Formal performance reviews are conducted as articulated by contracts and bargaining agreements. But all of us operate on another level of informal accountability to ourselves and to the school.

Above all, clear expectations convey assurance for all the members of the staff and demonstrate your confidence in them. During a time of change, expectations can be a steadying factor for all involved.

NOTES

_____

_____

_____

_____

_____

_____

_____

SELF-ASSESSMENT

A crucial aspect of moving to an ideal state is to gain a clear picture of the current state. Use the following needs assessment chart to determine areas of strength and growth opportunities for professional learning communities in the school or district you serve.

THE TEACHERS IN THIS SCHOOL/DISTRICT	
STATEMENT	PRIORITY (1 - 10)
1. **Use PLC teams to align with current professional learning goals and efforts.** None (0–10%)　　Some (11–50%)　　Most (51–89%)　　All (90–100%)	
2. **Routinely determine what it is that students already know to plan for student learning.** None (0–10%)　　Some (11–50%)　　Most (51–89%)　　All (90–100%)	
3. **Utilize teacher clarity processes to promote student learning.** None (0–10%)　　Some (11–50%)　　Most (51–89%)　　All (90–100%)	
4. **Consult current research on student learning to inform practice.** None (0–10%)　　Some (11–50%)　　Most (51–89%)　　All (90–100%)	
5. **Ground discussion of teaching in the context of student learning.** None (0–10%)　　Some (11–50%)　　Most (51–89%)　　All (90–100%)	
6. **Ground discussion of teaching in the context of its impact on student learning.** None (0–10%)　　Some (11–50%)　　Most (51–89%)　　All (90–100%)	
7. **Possess the communication skills needed to collaborate, not just cooperate.** None (0–10%)　　Some (11–50%)　　Most (51–89%)　　All (90–100%)	
8. **Examine how measures of equitable education are evidenced in their own classroom.** None (0–10%)　　Some (11–50%)　　Most (51–89%)　　All (90–100%)	
9. **Interrogate student learning results in the context of measures of equitable education.** None (0–10%)　　Some (11–50%)　　Most (51–89%)　　All (90–100%)	
10. **Continuously recalibrate their expectations using grade-level standards to plan.** None (0–10%)　　Some (11–50%)　　Most (51–89%)　　All (90–100%)	

PAUSE AND PONDER

Now that you have self-assessed, what are the current strengths that you can leverage? What are the growth opportunities?

Visit the companion website at
resources.corwin.com/PLC+forleaders
for downloadable resources.

NOTES

Idea 3

QUALITY QUESTIONS DRIVE THE DISCUSSIONS AND DECISIONS THAT TEAMS MAKE AS PART OF THE PLC+ PROCESS.

Essential Question: What discussion drivers are necessary for teams to assume collective responsibility for students' learning and support each other in continuous improvement?

PLC+ provides a framework for collaboration between and among teachers that allows them to engage in the necessary planning and implementation of student learning experiences that have an impact. This framework also ensures that the adults within the school continue their own professional learning journey. Five questions (Fisher et al., 2019a) drive the investigation cycle.

1. Where are we going?

2. Where are we now?

3. How do we move learning forward?

4. What did we learn today?

5. Who benefited and who did not benefit?

There is a story behind each of these questions and behind why these questions have been developed, refined, and implemented. These questions represent the next generation of PLC work that teams can accomplish together.

QUESTION 1: WHERE ARE WE GOING?

This is the foundation for every PLC+ team and conversation they have. This question focuses attention on the *intentions* for learning. It challenges us to move beyond pacing guides and curriculum maps to make clear-eyed decisions about the learning path we will blaze. Keep the end in mind: *What is it that we want our learners to know, understand, and be able to do?*

Keep the end in mind.

These intentions, of course, are not limited to content learning, and they can include language development and social and emotional learning outcomes. To achieve what they want in the classroom, teachers need clarity—a deep understanding about what to teach and why, how to teach it, and what success looks like. This goes beyond simply being familiar with the day's lesson. Moreover, it involves an ongoing process that enables teachers to deeply understand what is to be learned and to communicate those same aspects to their students.

The rigor level of the standard should remain constant, while the pathway for how students arrive at the mastery of the standard might look different. When PLC+ teams establish a consistent practice of reviewing standard expectations, pacing guides, and resources, the members develop a strong collaborative armor to learn and grow from each other. The unswerving focus is on promoting students' learning through careful analysis of their progress. The initial focus on analyzing the standards occurs so that teams can come to agreement on what will be taught and measured. This is only one-fifth of the inquiry cycle in the PLC+ framework. Although we "begin with the end in mind," the endpoint is the analysis of the impact on student learning.

PAUSE AND PONDER

Teacher clarity has an effect size of 0.85, which is well above average. This question, and the entire PLC+ process, is designed to ensure that all students are learning—not by chance but by design. How might this question ("*Where are we going?*") and the ones that follow foster clarity in and across classrooms?

QUESTION 2: WHERE ARE WE NOW?

What is the current level of student achievement and progress? This question drives home our belief that we must view learning with fluidity, not finality. It represents the start of a collective process for teams as they take inventory of student strengths and needs, analyze the data, and eventually determine solutions that will address the students' needs. PLC+ teams ground themselves in a collective process of determining a common challenge that is based on student needs evidenced by data. In the PLC+ framework, the term "common challenge" is the goal of what teams wish to accomplish; each PLC+ team, then, determines their own common challenge. Further, framing the team's goal as a *common challenge* is more inviting than *problem of practice* and distinguishes it from other goals established by the school and/or district.

> We must view learning with fluidity, not finality.

Each PLC+ team establishes a common challenge that is observable, actionable, and grounded in evidence. Having established learning intentions, success criteria, and learning progressions, PLC+ teams begin to engage in *initial assessment* of student learning through work samples, student interviews, and preassessments. Again, there is no point in teaching something that students already know. However, this particular question is prone to biases about student learning and particular groups of students. Thus, the effective navigation of this question requires us to be aware of those biases and recognize them when they infiltrate the PLC+ collaborative team meeting.

Assessment bias occurs because people are prone to selective perception, jumping on the bandwagon, and other anecdotal fallacies. Because of the sheer volume of data available, we may take mental shortcuts, or cognitive biases, when analyzing data. We may be selective about the data sources we choose, or we may draw conclusions based on a superficial understanding of the data, both of which can lead to mistaken beliefs and errors of judgment. The Assessment Network identifies six cognitive biases for educators to consider when analyzing assessments (Greenstein, 2019). Figure 3.1 defines these biases and provides an example for each.

NOTES

_____

_____

_____

_____

_____

_____

_____

_____

_____

FIGURE 3.1

COMMON TYPES OF ASSESSMENT BIASES

Confirmation Bias	Confirmation bias occurs when we search for additional evidence that confirms what we already believe to be true. *Example: The first-grade team briefly reviewed students' writing samples and concluded that students don't know letter sounds.*
Optimism Bias	Optimism bias occurs when we dismiss data because we want to believe students are doing well. *Example: A fifth-grade teacher says, "Each of my students took the test, and overall, they did great."*
Pessimism Bias	There is overconfidence and overemphasis on negative outcomes. *Example: A member of the third-grade team says, "They're never going to get it. Their families don't care."*
Reliance on Partial Information	A tendency to use prior knowledge and experience to draw conclusions. *Example: "He struggled in algebra last year, so he's not going to do well this year either."*
Illusion of Knowledge	The belief that we know more than we actually do. *Example: "I've taught first graders to read for ten years. I know how to do it."*
Status Quo Bias	The desire to maintain or return to one's comfort zone. *Example: "I just want to go back to the way we used to do it."*

PLC+ teams that embrace the core value of high expectations for all students must gather evidence of learners' knowledge about the skills and concepts students have yet to master. Awareness of biases during assessment analysis helps teams to be more objective; recommendations for reducing these biases are noted in Figure 3.2. A thorough understanding of student learning needs, coupled with high expectations, then prompts teachers to determine the knowledge students already bring to the learning experience, as well as to identify any current specific learning gaps that are present. A PLC+ team's ability to do this recaptures instructional time lost to teaching concepts students already know, and it helps the teachers build on students' assets to support a deeper level of learning.

FIGURE 3.2

RECOMMENDATIONS FOR REDUCING BIAS IN ASSESSMENT

1. Be clear on the success criteria for students from the beginning of each unit.

2. Students are involved in the direct monitoring of their learning progress so you're not the only one doing so. Learning accelerates when the student, not the teacher, is taught to be in control of the learning.

3. Make feedback part of a high-trust environment that is fully integrated into the learning cycle (not just at the end of the cycle).

4. Use a range of assessment and instruction approaches so that students can demonstrate their mastery in more than one way.

5. Know how to gauge your own impact on learning by using initial and confirmative assessments in tandem.

Source: Adapted from Fisher et al. (2021b).

PAUSE AND PONDER

Visit classrooms and notice if there are significant numbers of minutes devoted to learning that has already been accomplished by at least some of the students. How might focusing on this question help teachers increase the amount of time devoted to new learning?

Join team meetings when data is being analyzed. Are protocols for analyzing formal and informal data utilized? In what ways might teams be inadvertently taking mental shortcuts that cause bias in assessment?

QUESTION 3: HOW DO WE MOVE LEARNING FORWARD?

PLC+ teams should search for evidence-based actions that support moving the learning of *all* students forward.

Now that they know where they are headed, teams can tackle the question of how to get there. Once again, the wording of this question is intentional. PLC+ teams should search for evidence-based actions that support moving the learning of *all* students forward. Of course, this is a challenge. Teachers are bombarded with tricks, ideas, and strategies from many different sources. This third question requires PLC+ teams to assimilate the answers to the first two questions into a purposeful and intentional decision about effective learning strategies that move the learning needle for all students.

This requires discussion about which strategies are off limits because they are proven to be ineffective (e.g., round-robin reading, tracking). This forward movement could require PLC+ team members to engage in furthering their own professional learning. Then teams can focus on becoming informed about what actions are likely to work. When teams engage in understanding evidence-based instructional strategies, they are motivated and empowered to address the common challenge and measure their impact on learning.

PAUSE AND PONDER

When have we collectively avoided conversations about instructional strategies in professional learning community conversations? What negative consequences occur when teams fail to discuss instruction?

QUESTION 4: WHAT DID WE LEARN TODAY?

This question requires PLC+ collaborative teams to be reflective practitioners. Like other fields such as medicine and law, educators refer to their *practice*. Time for reflection and dialogue must be appropriated for PLC+ teams. Here teams examine evidence of learning, reflect on that aggregated and disaggregated evidence of learning, and then move forward with this evidence in mind. This particular question (*"What did we learn today?"*) can lead the group to focus on *impact*. There must be dialogue around the learning tasks they engineered, the strategies they used to support students in engaging in those tasks, and—as a result—how well students performed against the established learning intentions.

Did all students learn what they were supposed to learn? If not, why not? And if so, why? What actions and strategies should we replicate? Importantly, this question includes the word *today*. For us, this has many meanings. For the individual classroom teacher, the question begs for checking for understanding so that immediate action can be taken if some students did not learn. Team reflection can and should take student voices into account. For example, have our students told us they are still struggling to understand the concepts and skills we are focusing on? Do they need reteaching? Or have they shared they are close to the intended goals and targets but need practice and feedback? Both involve the need for PLC+ teams to budget time for reflective discussion about what they are learning from their students. In PLC+ teams, the process and pathway to respond to this question invite teachers into conversations about students' learning.

> Team reflection can and should take student voices into account.

PAUSE AND PONDER

What are effective and efficient ways for teachers to check for understanding? How often does this happen in the average classroom? What tools might be useful for teachers to learn and adopt?

QUESTION 5: WHO BENEFITED AND WHO DID NOT BENEFIT?

This final question in the PLC+ framework takes a critical look at challenging teams to consider their impact on all of their learners. Teams examine who did and did not make the expected learning gains as a result of instruction. And, to truly answer the question of benefit, we must refocus on the learning intentions, success criteria, and learning progressions that provide the definition of *benefit*. This creates an intentional cycle back to the first question: *"Where are we going?"* What makes Question 5 so vital to the PLC+ framework is also what makes this question challenging and at times uncomfortable: PLC+ teams must confront the evidence that points to learners who did not benefit from instruction.

In asking who benefited and who did not, PLC+ team members must explore trends and patterns in both the growth and achievement of all students. Are there common characteristics of learners not experiencing growth or achievement? This could support establishing supplemental and intensive interventions to provide equity of access and opportunity for all learners. Engaging in these conversations can surface teachers' limiting assumptions about the capabilities of students as well as barriers to learning (e.g., irrelevant learning experiences). Doing so can also help eliminate barriers to learning, especially when dedicated teachers identify these issues and then work to address them.

> This reflection will help reveal who is and who is not making those gains—and why they are not.

Reflecting on who did and who did not benefit will maintain our expectations for both growth and achievement, but at the same time, this reflection will help reveal who is and who is not making those gains—and *why* they are not. As part of this process, PLC+ teams focus tightly on identifying patterns among particular groups of learners, which may suggest underlying structural or institutional barriers to learning that are within our sphere of control. By identifying patterns and analyzing data, PLC+ teams are poised to take action and measure their impact. It's important to note that collective teacher efficacy (CTE) occurs only when teams analyze data, take action, and measure their impact. Skipping any of these components is unlikely to contribute to a team's CTE.

PAUSE AND PONDER

How can you help teams not abdicate responsibility for all students as they discuss this question? And why is it important for teachers—and teams of teachers—to know their impact on learning?

USING THE FIVE QUESTIONS

Because the PLC+ framework is an iterative process, the number of meetings does not need to correspond with the number of questions. For example, holding the first PLC+ meeting does not mean the team focuses only on the first question and that they must "finish" the first question by the end of the first meeting because the second PLC+ meeting is reserved for the second question. Instead, a team may spend two or three PLC+ meetings answering the first question, *"Where are we going?"* For example, if a particular set of skills or content is difficult and complex, then the team may need to devote more time to the development of learning intentions, success criteria, learning progressions, and their own professional learning around those skills and content. These conversations may continue in the hallway, teachers' workroom, or parking lot. The ultimate goal of the PLC+ framework is to use the five questions to facilitate dialogue about teaching and learning for all learners. Formal and informal discussions about teaching and learning should be the culture of every classroom, school, and district; ***plus***, the climate makes it feel right.

NOTES

SELF-ASSESSMENT

Use the following tool to assess the status of each question—and the thinking behind each question—in the school or district that you serve. Note that there is a reference to *The PLC+ Playbook* in the final column of this tool (Fisher et al., 2019b). If there is a team-specific need, protocols to support their work can be found in *The PLC+ Playbook*.

ACTIONS	REGULARLY	OCCASIONALLY	NEVER	*THE PLC+ PLAYBOOK MODULE*
1: Where are we going?				
Do your PLC+ teams collaboratively create learning intentions and success criteria using the skills and concepts in grade-level and content-area learning standards?				5
Do your PLC+ teams collaboratively determine critical learning progressions to drive the use of initial assessments for units of study?				5
2: Where are we now?				
Do your PLC+ teams gather and analyze student voice evidence as a driver of their actions and approaches?				7
Do your PLC teams develop and examine initial assessment evidence for an investigation cycle?				7
Do your PLC+ teams determine and act upon student misconceptions from initial evidence?				7–8
Do your PLC+ teams regularly examine assignments for alignment to their teacher clarity as well as for rigor level?				11
Do your PLC+ teams determine common challenges to prioritize areas that will have the greatest impact on student learning?				8
3: How do we move learning forward?				
Do your PLC+ teams use a process for determining instructional actions?				10
Do your PLC+ teams align instructional actions to the immediate needs of your students?				10

ACTIONS	REGULARLY	OCCASIONALLY	NEVER	THE PLC+ PLAYBOOK MODULE
Do your PLC+ team(s) tightly align their instructional actions to their assessment results?				10
Do teachers and school leaders engage in collaborative learning walks in your school/district?				12
Do teachers in your school/district engage in microteaching?				13
4: What did we learn today?				
Do your PLC+ teams intentionally reflect on *their* learning and impact as a team?				15
Do your PLC+ teams engage in any expert-noticing protocols?				16
Do your PLC+ teams acknowledge and determine how to address roadblocks for having deep, meaningful conversations about teaching and learning in PLC+ meetings?				19
What is the current reality related to your PLC+ teams' common assessment structure?				17
5: Who benefited and who did not benefit?				
Do your PLC+ teams engage in equity audits to determine if any patterns exist related to learning gaps with specific groups of students?				20
Do your PLC+ teams examine both progress and achievement with evidence and artifacts in PLC+ meetings?				21
Do your PLC+ teams align their work with your school's tiered systems of support?				21
Do your PLC+ teams take inventory of instructional actions and approaches for their Tier 2 and 3 interventions and supports?				21
Do your PLC+ teams monitor the level of quality and impact of tiered instructional actions?				21

After completing the chart, analyze your self-assessment. Which areas within the five guiding questions are most pressing to move your PLC+ teams forward toward your long-term vision? We've completed the first one as an example.

RANKING	QUESTION	RATIONALE	LEADERSHIP ACTION(S)	EVIDENCE OF SUCCESS
Example	3: How do we move learning forward?	I have gathered evidence to know that the PLC+ teams do not tightly align their instructional actions to their assessment results. Very often PLC+ team members jump directly to favorite activities rather than proven instructional strategies. Thus, alignment from intended targets and success criteria to instructional actions is minimal.	I will support the activators in identifying evidence-based strategies that they can use with their teams.	I will collect data from six to eight classrooms per week.
My #1				
My #2				
My #3				

Visit the companion website at
resources.corwin.com/PLC+forleaders
for downloadable resources.

Idea 4

THERE ARE SPECIFIC ENABLING CONDITIONS THAT ALLOW PROFESSIONAL LEARNING COMMUNITIES TO THRIVE.

Essential Question: What conditions are present in the teams at our school, and how can I identify leadership actions that promote effective and efficient teams?

We've focused on what does not work and what the next generation of PLCs needs to address if this structure is going to have an impact. Now it's time to identify the enabling conditions that allow PLCs to thrive. There are six evidence-based characteristics of PLCs (Hord, 2004). While the presence of these characteristics in and of themselves won't guarantee that a PLC is effective, they are important considerations that teams should discuss as they embark on the journey of improving student learning and teacher expertise.

Remember that the professional learning community is the school. We'll focus on the needs of specific teams later in this book. For now, take a moment to individually self-assess your current reality against each of the six characteristics listed in Figure 4.1, using the rating system below:

1. This is not yet established in our PLC.

2. This happens randomly and is not commonplace.

3. This exists but is not yet systematized.

4. This is systematically embedded within our PLC.

FIGURE 4.1

SIX ENABLING CONDITIONS OF A PROFESSIONAL LEARNING COMMUNITY

SIX CHARACTERISTICS OF AN EFFECTIVE PLC	CURRENT RATING
1. **Structural Conditions:** Does our PLC have established times when we are able to meet? Are there schedules in place that support collaboration and diminish isolation? Is there availability of needed resources?	1 2 3 4

Ideas for maintaining or strengthening this characteristic:

SIX CHARACTERISTICS OF AN EFFECTIVE PLC	CURRENT RATING
2. **Supportive Relational Conditions:** Is there trust and respect in place within our PLC that provides the basis for giving and accepting feedback in order to work toward improvement?	1 2 3 4

Ideas for maintaining or strengthening this characteristic:

SIX CHARACTERISTICS OF AN EFFECTIVE PLC	CURRENT RATING
3. **Shared Values and Vision:** Do members of the team have the same goal? Do they have shared beliefs about student learning and the ability of team members to impact student learning?	1 2 3 4

Ideas for maintaining or strengthening this characteristic:

SIX CHARACTERISTICS OF AN EFFECTIVE PLC	CURRENT RATING
4. Intentional Collective Learning: Does our PLC engage in discourse and reflection around sharing practices, knowledge, and skills to impact the growth and achievement of our students? Do we find ways to learn from each other or learn together?	1 2 3 4

Ideas for maintaining or strengthening this characteristic:

5. Peers Supporting Peers: Does our PLC support lifting each other up? Do we celebrate individual and group successes? Do we observe one another while engaged in practice to help others strengthen their practice?	1 2 3 4

Ideas for maintaining or strengthening this characteristic:

6. Shared and Supportive Leadership: Are power, authority, and decision making shared and encouraged between teachers and building leaders? Is there a positive relationship among administrators and teachers in the school, where all staff members grow professionally as they work toward the same goal?	1 2 3 4

Ideas for maintaining or strengthening this characteristic:

Source: Fisher et al. (2019b).

THE CLIMATE OF THE SCHOOL FOSTERS THESE CONDITIONS

Let's expand Hord's enabling conditions by linking them to the school climate. You'll recall from the introduction that we discussed the power of professional capital, which is a summation of the human, social, and decisional capital of the organization (Hargreaves & Fullan, 2012). The roots of these concepts are informed by the earlier work of Kruse et al. (1994) in examining the conditions that enabled school restructuring. They studied fifteen schools that enacted professional learning communities to learn about how the school's climate afforded or inhibited change. They noted that enabling conditions are unlikely to take root without professional capital, concluding that "If a school lacks the social and human resources to make use of those structural conditions, it's unlikely that a strong professional community can develop" and "the need to improve the culture, climate and interpersonal relationships in schools have received too little attention" (p. 6).

These attributes of high-performing professional learning communities are detailed in Figure 4.2. Notice the clear throughline of human, social, and decisional capital.

FIGURE 4.2

PROFESSIONAL CLIMATE OF SCHOOLS WHERE A PLC THRIVES

CRITICAL ELEMENTS OF SCHOOL CLIMATE	SOCIAL AND HUMAN RESOURCES	STRUCTURAL CONDITIONS
• Reflective dialogue	• Openness to improvement	• Time to meet and talk
• De-privatization of practice	• Trust and respect	• Physical proximity
• Collective focus on student learning	• Cognitive and skill base	• Interdependent teaching roles
• Collaboration	• Supportive leadership	• Communication structures
• Shared norms and values	• Socialization	• Teacher empowerment and school autonomy

Source: Adapted from the work of Kruse et al. (1994).

WHAT WENT WRONG? WHAT WENT RIGHT?

Read the following scenarios of PLC+ teams in action. Consider the optimal conditions for next-generation professional learning communities and the role leaders play in establishing those conditions. As you read through these scenarios, determine what leadership actions either would have promoted or could have prevented the scenario from coming to life. Also, consider how school climate and the six enabling conditions are reflected.

PLC+ TEAM 1

The sixth-grade team at West Middle School has been together for the past four years. They are a close-knit group, and most are friends both inside and outside of school. They often say they love their collaborative time, and any time the principal observes their meetings, they seem to be having fun and enjoying each other's company.

The leadership team, which includes both administrators as well as instructional coaches, has been much more intentional in monitoring the impact PLC+ teams are having on the achievement of students by examining the type of instructional dialogue occurring in meetings. Several other PLC+ teams at this school have learned to engage in meaningful conversations about instruction, and there is evidence of implementation. In contrast, the leadership team notes that this sixth-grade team rarely engages in any true, meaningful conversations related to instructional actions. They also note that there are several gaps between the actions that are agreed upon in their PLC+ meetings and what is actually happening in their classrooms. This sixth-grade team by far shows the biggest need for growth in both areas.

> **Leadership actions that would advance the team's effectiveness:**
>
>
>
> Which of the critical elements of school climate and six enabling conditions would be an appropriate focus for this team? Why?

PLC+ TEAM 2

The East High School science PLC+ team, which includes veteran educators and newer teachers, was formed fairly recently through the ownership of the teachers, who wanted to come together as a vertical team instead of as multiple teams organized by individual grade levels and specific courses (e.g., biology and chemistry). Their desire is to form a cohesive group to support students as they move from one grade level to the next in their science learning. School leaders have visited this team several times this semester.

Over the course of the year, the leadership team has gathered evidence on two specific areas to help determine the impact of the group's collaboration.

1. Degree of relational trust and collective responsibility

2. Assessment of growth and progress in student learning

The school leadership team engages with the staff several times through surveys to monitor the level of relational trust and collective responsibility present within all of the school's teams. In addition, the leadership team is striving to better align the capacity of teams to look at student achievement data gathered from assessment tools in order to take actionable steps. It is clear that the science team has developed a higher degree of relational trust during the year. Given this progress, the leadership team is looking to build on this improved trust by seeking to foster the science team's ability to collect and analyze data.

Leadership actions that would advance the team's effectiveness:

Which of the critical elements of school climate and six enabling conditions would be an appropriate focus for this team? Why?

PLC+ TEAM 3

The seventh-grade team at South Middle School is made up of what many observers would call *quiet doers*. They are strong, caring teachers who do their very best for students each and every day. They may not always be viewed as the most dynamic in their instructional actions, but they build solid relationships with students. While their achievement data are not the highest in the school or district, their students consistently make progress.

When they meet as a team, they are professional and collaborative but feel very constricted in their ability to have dialogue around new instructional approaches because their agendas are always dictated to them by school leadership. While they are happy to support anything they are asked to do—and they even appreciate a certain degree of structure for their meetings and cycles—this degree of rigidity has squelched any level of innovation and creativity the team might have experienced. They have begun to wonder how much more they would be able to impact student learning if they could devote specific time during their team meetings for learning and applying new instructional actions and approaches based on their students' learning needs. Collectively, they are becoming a compliance-based PLC+ team.

Leadership actions that would advance the team's effectiveness:

Which of the critical elements of school climate and six enabling conditions would be an appropriate focus for this team? Why?

PLC+ TEAM 4

From a distance, the academic support team at South Elementary could be described as a group that has embraced the PLC+ process as much as any team in the district. The team is very happy to meet on every one of their designated Wednesdays when time to do so is most structured and calendared. However, very little—if any—instructional dialogue takes place during those meetings because of the high level of freedom they are given.

Most of their time together is spent planning lessons for their students, many of whom are identified as in need of additional support because they are at risk of grade-level retention. This planning work is not anchored by teacher clarity (e.g., developing success criteria or examining assignments and tasks that align with success criteria). Instead, these meetings are very much about logistics (e.g., grading student work, planning lessons, or organizing instructional materials). The team performs these logistical tasks together in the room, and they get along very well. However, only rarely is there any instructional dialogue or analysis of barriers that impede learning and how to remove those barriers—the true work of a professional learning community.

Leadership actions that would advance the team's effectiveness:

Which of the critical elements of school climate and six enabling conditions would be an appropriate focus for this team? Why?

PLC+ TEAM 5

The PLC+ teams at Johnson Elementary School are thriving; we'll focus here on one team that comprises teachers from multiple grade levels. There are deep levels of collective efficacy that are driving team actions, and this team is oriented toward monitoring their impact on the learning of students. While members of this team teach different grade levels, they ensure they are allocating specific time in their meeting agendas to focus on the school's core practices and current professional learning elements—while being innovative and creative in their implementation at the same time.

Since this team is made up of educators who teach different grade levels, including veteran and novice teachers, the dynamics are intriguing. There are very different views among the group members related to instructional approaches, but they have developed a culture that allows for and even encourages debate and disagreement. However, they spend almost no time learning from one another outside of the structured meeting times. They rarely, if ever, are in each other's classrooms, and they have not developed skills for engaging in learning walks and microteaching.

Leadership actions that would advance the team's effectiveness:

Which of the critical elements of school climate and six enabling conditions would be an appropriate focus for this team? Why?

Now compare these teams with the ones at your school or district. You may have different teams that reflect each of the ones profiled in this section. Importantly, there are critical elements of school climate, enabling conditions, and leadership actions that can support teams to increase their collective efficacy and impact on learning. Next, we turn our attention to teacher credibility and collective efficacy.

Visit the companion website at
resources.corwin.com/PLC+forleaders
for downloadable resources.

Idea 5

HAVING A TIGHT-LOOSE-TIGHT MODEL ALLOWS FOR PURPOSE, AUTONOMY, AND MASTERY IN COLLABORATIVE MODELS OF TEACHER TEAMS.

Essential Question: How are you currently providing clarity of expectations as well as opportunities for both ownership and accountability in PLC+ teams?

Many school leaders adhere to a tight-loose model of leadership. *Tight* sometimes refers to nonnegotiable actions that provide teachers and teams clarity about the school's goals and about the actions that are expected to hold people accountable. *Loose* is usually associated with the ways teachers and teams can arrive at the goals or implement the actions expected.

A tight-loose approach allows individuals and teams a certain level of structured autonomy to choose their path to reach expected goals and targets. With this approach, leaders clearly communicate the vision, goals, and expected outcomes that teachers and teams are striving toward (tight). Teams are empowered by some room for innovation and creativity (loose) in how they accomplish those goals. Figure 5.1 contains examples of leaders' actions that are either tight or loose.

The dilemma of using only a tight-loose leadership stems from the fact that if we start with tight on the front end of a professional learning cycle and finish with loose, we may remain loose for a long time.

FIGURE 5.1

EXAMPLES OF TIGHT LEADERSHIP ACTIONS AND LOOSE LEADERSHIP ACTIONS

TIGHT LEADERSHIP ACTIONS	LOOSE LEADERSHIP ACTIONS
Asking teachers to create and share learning intentions and success criteria—and requiring teachers to align their lessons to these intentions and criteria—as their common challenge. (See Idea 6 for more specifics on developing common challenges.)	Empowering teachers to determine how they develop lessons and communicate learning intentions and success criteria to students. Empowering teachers to identify various ways to share learning intentions and success criteria with students.
Requiring PLC+ teams to collaboratively identify and implement effective evidence-based instructional strategies.	Empowering teachers to select any instructional tools that have evidence of impact and how they will be used in the classroom.
Using restorative practices as a method for promoting positive student behavior outcomes.	Empowering teachers and teams to determine the ways in which classroom meetings and circles are implemented.

PAUSE AND PONDER

Consider your school's or district's current approach to expected levels of implementation of professional learning goals. How have you communicated expected actions and outcomes? How are you monitoring and supporting teams to reach these outcomes? What was tight and what was loose?

BELIEFS ABOUT EMPLOYEES

McGregor (1960) created "Theory X" and "Theory Y" (see Figure 5.2) to explain management thinking. Theory X managers assume their employees are lazy and unmotivated, while Theory Y leaders assume their employees are self-motivating and ambitious. But here's the interesting thing, according to McGregor. If employees are placed in situations or organizations where they are assumed to be lazy and unmotivated, they are very likely to become lazy and unmotivated. The opposite happens if employees are assumed to be ambitious and self-motivating. Importantly, this self-fulfilling prophecy is used to justify either perspective about employees.

What does this have to do with our work on PLCs? Theory X leaders try to control everything and are very tight, whereas Theory Y leaders assume positive intent and are more likely to have tight and loose structures that guide the efforts of team members. In reality, the types of tasks and the amount of time allotted to those tasks likely influence the beliefs about employees and the actions leaders take (e.g., Morse & Lorsch, 1970). And it's rare for people to fit into dichotomous categories X versus Y; we probably are a combination of both. In response, Maslow (1969) suggested that there was an additional management theory: Theory Z, which suggests that leaders cultivate worker creativity, insight, meaning, and moral excellence.

NOTES

_____

_____

_____

_____

_____

_____

_____

_____

_____

_____

_____

_____

_____

_____

_____

FIGURE 5.2

ASPECTS OF THEORY X AND THEORY Y

 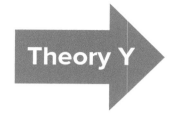

Attitude

We dislike work, find it boring, and will avoid it if we can.	**We need to work and want to take interest in it.** Under the right conditions, we can enjoy it.

Direction

We would rather be directed than accept responsibility, which we avoid.	**We will direct ourselves** toward a target that we accept.

Responsibility

We would rather be directed than accept responsibility, which we avoid.	**We will seek and accept responsibility** under the right considerations.

Motivation

We are motivated mainly by money and fears about our job security.	**Under the right conditions, we are motivated** by the desire to realize our own potential.

Creativity

Most of us have little creativity— except when it comes to getting around rules.	**We are highly creative creatures—**but are rarely recognized as such or given the opportunity to be.

TIGHT-LOOSE-TIGHT

Impact on student learning requires that what has been expected (tight) is supported, monitored, and comes to fruition. When the instructional leader fails to hold teams accountable for their impact, it's impossible to determine if the actions taken have led to students accomplishing the common challenge. Although there should be a great deal of freedom with the approaches teachers and teams take to reach the goals of their school or district (loose), leaders must ensure that autonomy drives the right degree of accountability on the back end so they can determine the impact these actions are having on student learning. Guthridge (2018) notes that when we engage teams in a tight-loose-tight approach, we position our teams to reach the holy grail of purpose, autonomy, and mastery.

We believe an approach that builds upon the merits of a tight-loose leadership model, as well as Theory Y and Theory Z, results in clarity of expected outcomes and opportunities for educators to seek and engage in peak, or mastery, experiences. Simply telling teams to develop success criteria to share with students (loose) might not be enough guidance for some PLC+ teams. Providing clear expectations (tight) for which actions they should take to progress toward the expected goals (tight)—as well as how they will be able to measurably support and monitor success—is equally important. Some examples of tight-loose-tight leadership in a PLC+ school can be found in Figure 5.3.

FIGURE 5.3

TIGHT-LOOSE-TIGHT LEADERSHIP IN A PLC+ SCHOOL

TIGHT LEADERSHIP ACTIONS ON THE FRONT END	LOOSE LEADERSHIP ACTIONS	TIGHT LEADERSHIP ACTIONS ON THE BACK END
Asking teachers to create and share learning intentions and success criteria—and requiring teachers to align their lessons to these intentions and criteria—as their common challenge. (See Idea 6 for more specifics on developing common challenges.)	Allowing teachers to determine how they develop lessons and communicate learning intentions and success criteria to students. Allowing teachers to identify various ways to share learning intentions and success criteria with students.	Monitor student understanding of learning intentions and success criteria through learning walks to collect data (see Idea 10 for a method for doing this).
Requiring PLC+ teams to collaboratively identify and implement effective evidence-based instructional strategies.	Allowing teachers to select any instructional tools that have evidence of impact and how they will be used in the classroom.	Requiring PLC+ teams to collect evidence of impact through initial and summative assessments (see Idea 13 for more gauging progress and achievement).
Using restorative practices as a method for promoting positive student behavior outcomes.	Allowing teachers and teams to determine the ways in which classroom meetings and circles are implemented.	Requiring PLC+ teams to analyze who is benefiting and who is not to address structural or institutional barriers (see Idea 10 for more on collecting data to analyze trends).

As a leader, how are you intentionally communicating and monitoring the degree to which what is tight is tight and what is loose is loose? What measurable indicators of adult actions and student outcomes do you plan to monitor in the next four to six weeks?

SELF-ASSESSMENT

Use the following chart to identify your school's or district's three highest priorities for your PLC+ team process to develop and implement during the next twelve to twenty-four months.

PRIORITIES	WHAT IS TIGHT IN TERMS OF EXPECTED ACTIONS OF THE ADULTS/PLC+ TEAMS? (CONSIDER SPECIFIC ACTIONS IN TERMS OF DEGREE AND FREQUENCY.)	WHAT IS LOOSE IN TERMS OF THE FREEDOM OF TEACHERS AND TEAMS TO BE INNOVATIVE AND CREATIVE IN THEIR IMPLEMENTATION?	WHAT IS TIGHT ON THE BACK END FOR MONITORING MEASURABLE OUTCOMES AND DETERMINING IMPACT?
First Priority			
Second Priority			
Third Priority			

Visit the companion website at
resources.corwin.com/PLC+forleaders
for downloadable resources.

NOTES

Idea 6

TEAMS NEED A GOAL, WHICH WE CALL THE *COMMON CHALLENGE,* IN PLC+ WORK.

Essential Question: What are the challenges that teachers face when it comes to student learning, and how might they collaborate to address those challenges?

Teams seem to work better when they have a common goal (e.g., Cockerell, 2008). A shared goal serves as a public acknowledgment of the team's direction, and it allows team members to allocate their resources, including time and effort, to achieving the goal. With that in mind, leaders should not simply impose a goal on teams; this action compromises the commitment that some members will have to achieving the goal. When team members develop and agree on a shared goal, there is an increased likelihood that everyone will work toward achieving it.

In the PLC+ framework, we focus on a common challenge that serves as the goal that the team wants to accomplish. We use the term *common challenge* instead of *problem of practice* or *SMART goal* because it is more inviting. Essentially, it indicates something that a group of educators has in common, and it identifies a current, relevant challenge that they want to solve.

Much like the learning pit (Nottingham, 2017), which illustrates the role of struggle as a necessary component of student learning, the change model of Satir et al. (2006) suggests that when teams of adults work together, there is some struggle, perhaps resistance, and ideally some transformational ideas that allow the team to identify and implement a new status quo. (See Figure 6.1 for a visual of this process.) It's important for leaders to note that there is a natural dip, sometimes called the *implementation dip,* which is defined as "a dip in performance and confidence as one encounters an innovation that requires new skills and new understandings" (Fullan, 2001, p. 40). The implementation dip temporarily lowers performance before raising it above previous levels. If leaders interfere too early in this change process, then educators may be left at the bottom of the dip and miss the opportunity to work through the challenge and achieve new levels of success.

FIGURE 6.1

WHEN TEAMS TAKE ON A CHALLENGE

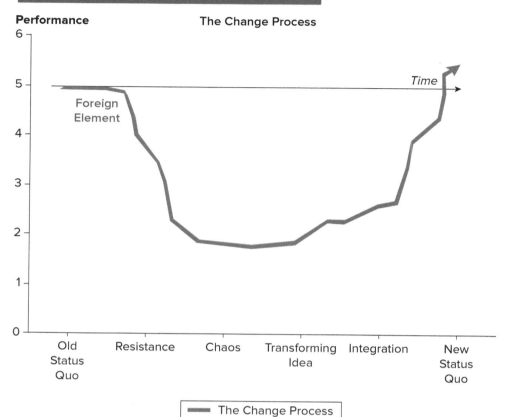

Performance

The Change Process

Time

Foreign Element

6

5

4

3

2

1

0

Old Status Quo | Resistance | Chaos | Transforming Idea | Integration | New Status Quo

—— The Change Process

PAUSE AND PONDER

Have you ever experienced the implementation dip as you worked on a team? How did you and the team negotiate the dip? How long did it take? How did you recover?

When teams understand where they are going and where they are now, they identify gaps. Often, there are many gaps, and any one of them could serve as the common challenge.

PAUSE AND PONDER

What has been your experience with developing a common challenge?

When educators share and collectively identify common concerns or sets of problems, the process ignites both their efforts and their passions to deepen their knowledge and expertise through ongoing interaction toward a common goal (Wenger et al., 2002). For example, a team of kindergarten teachers identified a gap between what their students needed to learn and what they already knew. They noted that most students' letter formation while writing was below developmental expectations. They also saw that most students had a hard time rereading what they had written and seemed to tell listeners about their writing from memory instead of looking at the page. In addition, they witnessed students who did not have good control of spaces between words.

There are a number of common challenges that the team could have developed from these data points. What's important is that this group of teachers agreed on a robust common challenge and then set forth to address that challenge. In this case, they decided that their challenge was "Our students' limitations in letter formation are contributing to their difficulty in reading what they have written."

PAUSE AND PONDER

Have you ever experienced the implementation dip as you worked on a team? How did you and the team negotiate the dip? How long did it take? How did you recover?

A QUALITY COMMON CHALLENGES CHECKLIST

The common challenge likely does not span a year; one annual investigation is likely too broad and too vague. It doesn't allow for the PLC+ team to revise their common challenge in the face of new data. Rather, a common challenge might last six to nine weeks so that there is a starting and ending point to each cycle. This allows the teacher team to revisit their progress more frequently and shape their next common challenge based on what they have learned. We use the following guide to identify a common challenge. The common challenge should meet these criteria.

- ☐ It's grounded in the evidence we gather during the *"Where are we now?"* phase.

- ☐ It's observable and actionable.

- ☐ It should make a significant difference in students' learning if acted upon.

- ☐ It's something the team is curious about.

- ☐ It should mobilize and motivate teachers to engage in the work required to meet the goals they have for themselves and their students.

Figure 6.2 contains examples and non-examples of common challenges.

FIGURE 6.2

COMMON CHALLENGES

EXAMPLES OF STUDENT LEARNING COMMON CHALLENGES	NON-EXAMPLES OF STUDENT LEARNING COMMON CHALLENGES
Students are not able to utilize advanced verbal reasoning skills to comprehend grade-level texts.	School garden
Students are learning about claims-evidence-reasoning in English courses but not applying the technique in other disciplines.	Homework
	Students from low-socioeconomic homes
The results of our study skills survey show that students have a limited understanding of techniques and their effects on learning.	English learners
	Student apathy
Students require a higher degree of writing fluency than currently seen in their composition of short constructed responses.	Reading comprehension
Students are having difficulty applying logic and reasoning to determine the underlying structures of complex mathematic problems that contain relevant and irrelevant information.	

Leaders can help PLC+ teams create common challenges that will drive their learning by relating them to school or district professional development initiatives.

Leaders can help PLC+ teams create common challenges that will drive their learning by relating them to school or district professional development initiatives. This is a great way to ensure that teacher teams in the professional learning community are provided with structure and guidance as well as a certain level of freedom to develop mastery-learning experiences of key and expected practices. Leaders should then have teams commit to certain periods of time in PLC+ meetings to focus on their own learning, such as a six- to nine-week cycle. For example, a *tight* approach might be directing teams to focus at least three meetings during the first quarter on collaboratively developing learning intentions and success criteria. A *loose* approach might be allowing teams to determine how and when they will do so. Then the *tight* approach for the end of the cycle might be expecting them to share their reflections on their impact with the schoolwide professional learning community.

Once the team has collaboratively determined a common challenge, they turn their attention to ways to meet that challenge. The obvious place to start is instruction. In some PLC models, teams are discouraged from discussing instruction because there is a fear that teachers may be told how to teach or because the focus might shift from learning to teaching. The PLC+ model encourages conversations about instructional innovation because teachers need time to share their practices with one another (Timperley, 2011). It's important to note that the practices should have some evidence of impact, and the team should collect evidence to determine whether or not the practice worked for their students.

PAUSE AND PONDER

How will you make sure that the common challenges are effectively addressed? How will you monitor teams' collaboration without micromanaging them? What evidence will you collect? How frequently?

THE COMMON CHALLENGE PROTOCOL

In Figure 6.3, we focus on the ways in which teams can identify their common challenge. The protocol is from the *PLC+ Playbook* (Fisher et al., 2019b). We also note the leadership moves and supports necessary to ensure that this process is successful.

FIGURE 6.3

COMMON CHALLENGE PROTOCOL AND LEADERSHIP MOVES

COMMON CHALLENGE PROTOCOL	LEADERSHIP MOVES
IDENTIFYING POSSIBLE COMMON CHALLENGES (UP TO 25 MINUTES)	
Getting Started: Identify an activator for this protocol. Assign a timekeeper and, if desired, a recorder. Also assign a presenter. (Because the activator is assisting the team in moving the discussion forward, we advise choosing another person to serve as the presenter.)	• Ensure that there is a trained activator who can lead the process. • Meet with the presenter(s) in advance, if needed, to help them identify evidence that they can use to suggest a common challenge.
Step 1 (5 minutes): The presenter shares the common challenge and describes the following: • Where it came from, who was involved in identifying it, and its connection to data • Context of other school or district efforts to address the problem	• Allow the team to process the information. • Observe and monitor if the team is new to this process.

Step 2 (5 minutes): Team members ask factual clarifying questions.	• Provide question frames that focus on clarifying questions versus other types of questions. Examples to use include
	
	  o Is this what you said . . . ?
	  o Did I hear you say . . . ?
	  o Did I understand you when you said . . . ?
	  o What criteria did you use to . . . ?
	  o What's another way you might . . . ?
	  o Did I hear you correctly when you said . . . ?
	  o Did I paraphrase what you said correctly?

Step 3 (8 to 10 minutes): The presenter steps back (remains silent) while team members provide the following. • **Warm feedback:** Aspects of the common challenge that—based on the criteria and list of potential challenges—make them think this will work well to address student needs • **Cool feedback:** Concerns or questions about the common challenge, including tuning suggestions • **Stretches:** Other things the presenter may not have thought about, but that might support the goals of the PLC+	• Provide facilitation skills, as needed, for team members to engage in warm and cool feedback as well as stretches. • Observe and monitor if the team is new to this process. • Participate in the process, especially if the common challenge being discussed is unlikely to impact student learning.

(Continued)

(Continued)

COMMON CHALLENGE PROTOCOL	LEADERSHIP MOVES
IDENTIFYING POSSIBLE COMMON CHALLENGES (UP TO 25 MINUTES)	
Step 4 (balance of 25 minutes' time): The presenter rejoins for general discussion, while the activator engages in a discussion, including • Responses and factual clarifications by the presenter • Feedback from team members that is focused on supporting the common challenge and that is not to be taken personally. It is not an evaluation of an individual teacher, but rather a collective brainstorm to respond to the common challenge • Reflections by all participants about what they learned	• Observe and monitor if the team is new to this process. • Ensure that there is a trained activator who can lead the process.
REACHING CONSENSUS ON THE COMMON CHALLENGE (UP TO 15 MINUTES)	
Step 1: Consider the possible common challenges. • What are the relative strengths of and barriers to each? • How does each possible challenge rate on the characteristics of common challenges quality checklist?	• Observe and monitor if the team is new to this process. • Trust the process.

Step 2: Propose a common challenge.
 	
• Members formulate a proposed common challenge, amending it to reflect the discussion.
 	
• Members work together to solve problems and fine-tune the proposed common challenge.
 	
• Test for agreement among members:
 	
   ○ I will fully support our inquiry cycle investigating this common challenge.
   ○ I am in support of my colleagues' decision.
   ○ I will not block this decision.
	• Contribute to the discussion, as appropriate, especially in the fine-tuning of the language in the common challenge.
	
	• Avoid critiques of the common challenge as long as it is likely to positively impact student learning.
	
	• Note the levels of agreement and which staff members do and do not agree. There may be implications for the future development of their collective efficacy (see Idea 8).

Step 3: The activator asks, "Are there any further questions or concerns about the common challenge we have selected?" If there is no further discussion, then agreement has been reached. If there is a call of concern, the person raising the concern reexamines by repeating Steps 1 and 2.	• Observe and monitor if the team is new to this process. • Trust the process.
Step 3: Debrief the protocol. • Plus/delta on the protocol itself: What did the group do well? What could have been improved?	• Observe and monitor if the team is new to this process. • Trust the process. • Make notes about refinements for future processes for the common challenge protocol.

Source: Adapted from Fisher et al. (2019b).

SELF-ASSESSMENT

A team of middle school teachers representing different content areas but teaching the same grade level reviewed the data from an interim assessment and noted that students' vocabulary scores are below grade-level expectations. As one of the team members shared, "Across the board, academic vocabulary is weak, but I am also thinking about student motivation. I don't think teaching a bunch of words is going to help. I think we need to focus more on projects across our content areas." A peer in the group added, "That would be interesting. I think we could develop some cool projects and problem-based learning units that would be fun for students."

As their conversation continued, the team decided that their common challenge would be to "design a project for students in our content areas" and that they would meet regularly to update one another about the progress of their projects. As one of them noted, "I'm not sure what kind of project I'll have students do, but I'm thinking that maybe illustrating the ideas in the chapters we're reading might help them understand the text. They could then share their illustrations with each other and teach each other what's in the text."

Considering the decisions this team made, analyze the situation against the conditions previously presented about common challenges.

COMMON CHALLENGE CONDITIONS	DOES THIS SITUATION MEET THE CONDITION?
It's grounded in the evidence we gather during the *"Where are we now?"* phase.	
It's observable and actionable.	
It should make a significant difference in students' learning if acted upon.	
It's something the team is curious about.	
It should mobilize and motivate teachers to engage in the work required to meet the goals they have for themselves and their students.	

Visit the companion website at
resources.corwin.com/PLC+forleaders
for downloadable resources.

NOTES

Idea 7

PROFESSIONAL LEARNING OPPORTUNITIES SHOULD BE ALIGNED WITH, AND COMPLEMENTARY TO, THE WORK TEACHERS ARE DOING IN THEIR PROFESSIONAL LEARNING COMMUNITIES.

Essential Question: How can the school's or district's professional learning calendar of offerings consider teachers' desired learning?

As educators of children and adolescents, we need to remember that adults learn differently than children. It's not effective to simply replicate practices used with students because adult learners come with their own set of experiences and want to have input about their next steps as learners. Knowles (1990) reminds us there are four principles of teaching adults (andragogy). He suggests that instructional leaders should be mindful that

- Adults want to be involved in the planning and assessment of their learning.

- Experience, even mistakes, is a valued part of the learning process.

- Adults are keenly interested in learning subjects that have immediate relevance and impact in their profession.

- Adults prefer learning that is problem-oriented, rather than content-centered.

With these principles in mind, instructional leaders can optimize the professional learning of educators by being open to approaches that align with adult learning theory. One way to apply this theory is to have PLC+ teams determine their common challenge, which will guide them to select their professional learning topics and strategies. As we know, teaching is complex, and educators develop expertise over the course of their careers; we don't learn everything we need to know in teacher-credentialing programs. As instructional leaders, we strive to promote lifelong learning and develop the cognitive flexibility to adjust instruction to ensure all students' success.

Although teachers often profess to be lifelong learners, there are misconceptions about how time is used. Specifically, some teams use their team time to share lesson plans or vent about student behavior or other administrative matters. Sometimes, instructional leaders use the time as a staff meeting or as a time for mandatory training. In fact, it's often the first thing cut when we're short on time.

PLC+ time is optimally used when teachers discuss tools for learning and their impact on student learning.

PRESERVING THE LEARNING IN A PROFESSIONAL LEARNING COMMUNITY

Although other issues and priorities may arise, we believe that PLC+ time is sacred. PLC+ time is optimally used when teachers discuss tools for learning and their impact on student learning. In other words, true PLC+ teams keep the L in PLC as the primary focus.

Unfortunately, *teachers* have been missing from the professional learning community. We don't mean their attendance or even their cognitive engagement, but rather the fact that recent models of PLC have been almost exclusively focused on students and what they are or are not learning. What we hear in these models is "It's all about the kids." And yes, student learning is critical, but the origins of professional learning communities recognize that adults need to continue to learn so that their students can learn. Keeping student learning at the forefront requires that we also recognize the vital role that educators play in the equation of teaching and learning. This means that instructional leaders must take on two additional challenges:

1. Maximizing teachers' individual expertise

2. Harnessing the power of the collaborative expertise that can develop within a PLC+ team

To accomplish this, leaders need to be aware of the characteristics of professional development versus professional learning (see Figure 7.1). In other words, professional development is done to you, while professional learning is done with and by you. Note the ways in which learning differs from the idea that others can develop you.

FIGURE 7.1

DIFFERENCES BETWEEN PROFESSIONAL DEVELOPMENT AND PROFESSIONAL LEARNING

CHARACTERISTICS OF PROFESSIONAL DEVELOPMENT	CHARACTERISTICS OF PROFESSIONAL LEARNING
• "One-and-done"	• Self-directed
• "Drive-by"	• Learning can be implemented tomorrow
• District-mandated	• Choice and input from participants
• Lack of buy-in	• Relevant and connected to current challenges
• Disconnected from current realities in classrooms	• Connected to specific content and/or standards
• No educator input	• Includes models and coaching
• Not necessarily oriented to school goals	• Is of sustained duration
	• Is aligned to school goals and standards

Source: Adapted from Scherff (2018).

PAUSE AND PONDER

Thinking of your own school, describe what adult learning looks like on a regular basis. Is it more on the professional development side or the professional learning side? What actions might you take to enhance the professional learning culture?

Idea 7: Professional learning opportunities should be aligned with the work teachers are doing in their PLCs.

67

TYPES OF PROFESSIONAL LEARNING

Professional learning can take many forms and is not limited to time in an auditorium or library with someone talking, although we have each learned in that type of situation—especially when the presenter was credible and encouraged us to interact with the ideas and each other. Figure 7.2 includes a summary of the characteristics of effective presentations of information.

FIGURE 7.2

CHARACTERISTICS OF EFFECTIVE PRESENTATIONS

CHARACTERISTIC	ELEMENTS
Social equity	• Uses inclusive examples • Uses nonbiased language
Presentation skills	• Is knowledgeable, current, and accurate in the subject • Uses examples that are relevant and meaningful to participants • Is verbally fluent, with good public-speaking skills
Motivation	• Arouses a sense of curiosity among students • Stimulates student interest • Presents the material in interesting ways
Modeling	• Shows enthusiasm for the subject and the participants • Is an academic role model
Mode of lecture	• Paces the lecture to allow participants to take notes • Provides summaries throughout
Critical thinking	• Encourages independence in learning • Challenges participants' views of the world to stimulate critical reasoning
Cognitive processes	• Has a clear structure • Builds on participants' prior and background knowledge • Pauses so that participants can consolidate their thinking

Source: Adapted from Fisher et al. (1998).

Use the information in Figure 7.2 to screen potential presenters, or use it to evaluate the presentations. If you are a presenter yourself, video record a presentation you make and then consider the ways in which you addressed each of the characteristics.

Social Equity: _____

Presentation Skills: _____

Motivation: _____

Modeling: _____

Mode of Lecture: _____

Critical Thinking: _____

Cognitive Processes: _____

LEARNING WALKS

Beyond the traditional learning experiences such as presentations, teachers can learn from visiting the classrooms of their peers and engaging in learning walks. This is not the time to evaluate or assess others, but rather an opportunity to see how students are responding to the instruction, specifically the impact that it has on learning.

An important hallmark of successful professional learning communities is that members carve out time to spend with one another in their respective classrooms. Keep in mind that PLC+ teams are *not* groups that meet only on early release days. The heartbeat of a PLC+ rests in the quality time members invest in one another, engaged in inquiry about their practices and the impact of their efforts. Time spent in each other's classrooms is an essential part of this equation.

Learning walks are an effective method for exploring common challenges identified by a PLC+. In their scope and formality, learning walks differ from instructional rounds (City et al., 2009), which use protocols for establishing long-term networks, defining problems of practice, and formally analyzing patterns based on a problem of practice. Comparatively, learning walks are more loosely structured, involve short-term team formations, and utilize different protocols. Protocols for learning walks are featured in *The PLC+ Playbook* (Fisher et al., 2019b).

> Professional development is done to you, while professional learning is done with and by you.

Learning walks require professional learning and practice. For example, teachers engaging in learning walks must learn to discern between descriptive and evaluative statements. Descriptive statements are neutral and objective observations (e.g., "learning intentions and success criteria were posted in all three classrooms") while evaluative ones interject an opinion (e.g., "I liked the way the teacher . . ." or "The teacher should have . . ."). Evaluative statements do not have a place in learning walks, as they shut down the ability of the team to generate ideas. Evaluative statements can also undermine the relational trust that PLC+ teams need to thrive.

Learning walks are most effective when they are aligned with the PLC+ teams' agreed common challenge. In some cases, the host teacher may determine an aspect of the common challenge; in others, it is jointly determined by the PLC+. In the following section, we will briefly review several types of learning walks that teams can use to engage in professional learning.

Ghost walks. Visiting empty classrooms is a great way to conduct a learning walk, especially for PLC+ teams that have not conducted learning walks before. We call these *ghost walks,* since students—and sometimes the classroom teacher—are not present during these observations (Fisher et al., 2019b). PLC+ members make their classrooms available during a prep period and also participate in the ghost walk, where the observation is confined to discussion about the physical environment. As an example, when Prairie View Elementary School was focused on getting better at communicating learning intentions and success criteria to students, teachers in the primary grades PLC+ teams used a ghost walk to see how the environment was being used to accomplish this with their students.

Capacity-building learning walks. Some learning walks are conducted expressly for the purpose of gathering evidence to inform decisions, which we call a *capacity-building learning walk* (Fisher et al., 2019b). For example, the PLC+ teams at Prairie View Elementary use capacity-building learning walks with novice teachers and teachers who are new to the school. PLC+ colleagues are paired with the new teachers so they can discuss how PLC+ efforts are evidenced in classrooms.

On one occasion, a veteran teacher, Ms. Laverne, accompanied a new first-grade teacher, Jaime Rubalcaba, on a capacity-building learning walk that was focused on teacher modeling of expert thinking. Here's how they summarized their experience.

"Mr. Rubalcaba wasn't really familiar with teacher modeling when he arrived here at Prairie View," explained Ms. Laverne. "So, we went to three classrooms during rotations, when our students were at art or PE. It was prearranged, and he got to see three teachers doing a think-aloud to model their expert thinking in real time."

Mr. Rubalcaba added, "It helped me tremendously. I've read transcripts of think-alouds, but seeing the interactions between the teacher and the students gave me a better sense of it. I'll be trying it out tomorrow."

As another example, the third- and fifth-grade teachers at Falcon Ridge Elementary School conducted a capacity-building learning walk with Alicia Sandoval, a member of the fourth-grade PLC+, to learn more about the logistics of dyad reading. The third- and fifth-grade teachers were energized by the findings shared by their fourth-grade colleagues on pairing readers to jointly read more complex texts, but they still had questions regarding implementation. After the walk, one third-grade teacher said, "It's actually simpler than I imagined, and it was helpful to talk with a few students about their impressions."

PAUSE AND PONDER

What advantages are there to having learning walks as part of your professional learning culture?

Thinking of your PLC+ teams, what needs to be in place for teams to feel comfortable trying out one or both of these types of learning walks?

USING MICROTEACHING TO IMPROVE TEACHING AND LEARNING

Microteaching—the practice of using a video clip to discuss the thinking behind a lesson or the implementation of an evidence-based strategy—is one of the most effective ways to improve teaching and learning. Figure 7.3 identifies what microteaching is and is not. Importantly, teachers film one of their own lessons that address the common challenge and then select a few minutes of the video to share with other team members. As they watch the video, the participants benefit from hearing the thinking of the teacher as the lesson progresses, which would be nearly impossible to accomplish during a walkthrough. It also provides teachers an opportunity to consider the questions and wondering of peers about the part of the lesson they've selected, which makes it a really powerful tool to help the team learn from each other.

FIGURE 7.3

DEFINING MICROTEACHING

WHAT MICROTEACHING IS		WHAT MICROTEACHING IS NOT
To co-construct content pedagogical knowledge with the team	**Purpose**	To evaluate someone else's teaching
Identified by the teacher	**Determination of Focus**	Identified by others
Directs the discussion	**Role of the Teacher**	Listens passively
To ask mediating questions to prompt the thinking of the teacher	**Role of Other PLC+ Members**	To provide feedback about the quality of the lesson, to offer judgments and personal opinions

Source: Adapted from Fisher et al. (2019b).

Importantly, there is strong evidence that microteaching works. Microteaching has an effect size of 0.88, more than double the average impact on all the things we do in schools (Visible Learning Meta[X], 2021; www.visiblelearningmetax.com). It seems reasonable to suggest that microteaching should be more common in schools. However, simply video-recording classrooms is not going to result in the impact noted in research. Instead, the video must be used as the discussion tool to encourage team members to notice the moves they are making in relation to the common challenge as well as the impact those moves have on student learning.

The PLC+ Playbook (Fisher et al., 2019b) contains a protocol for microteaching. The questions that are used to foster the discussion are very important so that the experience does not turn into a critique or evaluation. Questions we use include the following:

- What did you want your students to know and be able to do?

- What connections have you made?

- What did you see or hear that confirms your previous thinking?

- What did you see or hear that conflicts with your previous thinking?

- Which moments did you find to be particularly effective?

- Which moments did you think did not go as well as you had hoped?

- What was different in comparing those moments?

- What would you change to accomplish your stated goal?

- What do you want to be sure to do again?

PAUSE AND PONDER

The willingness to record yourself, and model the vulnerability required of teachers who engage in microteaching, often provides a powerful model that stokes a culture of feedback. How might you plan a lesson, deliver that experience for students, and then share your thinking with a group of teachers?

Idea 7: Professional learning opportunities should be aligned with the work teachers are doing in their PLCs.

73

GOALS OF PROFESSIONAL LEARNING AND PROFESSIONAL LEARNING COMMUNITIES

Effective PLCs support teachers in knowing what to do in the context of individual and collective efficacy, expectations, equity, and the facilitation of learning—both for students and for staff. We hold the following beliefs about the structure and function of teams as they work collaboratively to improve student learning.

1. We must keep the equity of access and opportunity to learn at the forefront of each PLC+ collaborative team meeting.

2. We must ensure that the dialogue provoked by the five questions is facilitated in such a way that the work of the PLC+ is not hindered or impeded.

3. We must develop learning experiences that make our expectations for learning clear to all students.

NOTES

_____

_____

_____

_____

_____

_____

_____

_____

_____

_____

_____

_____

_____

_____

_____

SELF-ASSESSMENT

Assess the current state of professional learning at your school site or district. Use the following rating scale to determine your thinking about frequency and quality.

1: This condition is not present.

2: This condition is rarely present.

3: This condition is often, although not always, present.

4: This condition is fully integrated into decisions about and design of professional learning.

HIGH-QUALITY AND EVIDENCE-BASED PROFESSIONAL LEARNING STRATEGIES	RATING SCALE	EVIDENCE OF VALUE: HOW IS THIS CHARACTERISTIC OBSERVED OR EXPERIENCED?	NOTES
Focuses on the content students need to know as it relates to the goals of the professional community (that is, content standards, key curriculum concepts, assessments)	1 2 3 4		
Contributes to teacher pedagogical content knowledge (PCK) in areas aligned with goals	1 2 3 4		
Provides sufficient time, opportunities, and support for building efficacy and mastery of new PCK	1 2 3 4		
Aligns with principles of andragogy in terms of active learning	1 2 3 4		
Involves participants working in meaningful collaborative groups to hone learning	1 2 3 4		

(Continued)

Idea 7: Professional learning opportunities should be aligned with the work teachers are doing in their PLCs.

75

(Continued)

HIGH-QUALITY AND EVIDENCE-BASED PROFESSIONAL LEARNING STRATEGIES	RATING SCALE	EVIDENCE OF VALUE: HOW IS THIS CHARACTERISTIC OBSERVED OR EXPERIENCED?	NOTES
Brings together educators who are already associated in some manner (that is, PLC+ teams, vertical teams, content areas, issues, or leadership roles)	1 2 3 4		
Intentionally develops a sense of community, interspersing face-to-face experiences with online experiences as appropriate	1 2 3 4		
Involves initial and follow-up opportunities for learning and long term; ongoing contact with colleagues, coaches, and leaders	1 2 3 4		
Embedded within the school day or school year	1 2 3 4		
Applies or situates professional learning in teachers' classrooms so they can learn on the job and try out ideas directly related to their curriculum	1 2 3 4		
Provides opportunities for analyzing and reflecting on practice and learning from evidence-based feedback	1 2 3 4		

Source: Adapted from the U.S. Department of Education, Office of Educational Technology (2014).

Visit the companion website at
resources.corwin.com/PLC+forleaders
for downloadable resources.

Idea 8

THERE IS A STRONG RELATIONSHIP BETWEEN TEACHER CREDIBILITY AND COLLECTIVE TEACHER EFFICACY (AND BOTH ARE IMPORTANT FOR PLCs TO FUNCTION WELL).

Essential Question: What is my role as a leader in developing teacher credibility and fostering collective teacher efficacy?

As noted previously, there are many benefits to students and educators when the adults work together toward a shared goal. In this section, we focus on teacher credibility and collective teacher efficacy, both of which have strong influences on student learning. However, these two constructs are both ongoing, multifaceted, and interrelated. Since credibility and collective teacher efficacy are not skills that are easily mastered and replicated, these are topics that teams should attend to year after year.

TEACHER CREDIBILITY: FOUR ASPECTS THAT LEAVE LASTING IMPRESSIONS ON STUDENTS

Teacher credibility is an interesting influence on learning, in that it is a measure of a student's perception that they can learn from this adult. In other words, we don't get to decide that we are credible to students—they do. Because teacher credibility has a strong influence on academic achievement, it's important to know the four aspects that comprise teacher credibility and how each works:

- Trustworthiness

- Competence

- Dynamism

- Immediacy

In this section, we will explore these elements in more detail because each contributes to students' beliefs that they can learn from the educators in their school. In fact, the effect size for teacher credibility is 1.09, well worth the effort it takes to improve this (Visible Learning Meta^X, 2021, www.visiblelearningmetax.com).

PAUSE AND PONDER

You likely remember an educator who made a positive lasting impression on you. Take a moment to think of that individual and consider what made that person so special to you. Was it perhaps that you felt seen and heard for the first time? Perhaps this teacher made learning exciting. Whatever the reason(s), it's likely this educator had a high degree of teacher credibility. Who was that person for you? In what ways did this person contribute to your learning?

TRUSTWORTHINESS

A popular adage is that *trust takes time to build, is easy to lose, and is difficult to repair*. This is because trusting relationships require an emotional investment; they involve more than just knowing each of our students' names. Instead, students learn to trust and rely on us as their teachers when our actions align with our words. Elements of trustworthiness include reliability, honesty, openness to feedback from students, and benevolence, which is a student's view that "the educator has my best interests at heart" (Hoy & Tschannen-Moran, 2003).

COMPETENCE

Another aspect of trust is competence. This is often perceived as a given, but it also implies that an educator knows how to organize, sequence, and deliver instruction in ways that make sense to the current students (not students from a past year). Competence involves not only subject matter knowledge but also the ability to convey learning to novices. Some of us have been in the company of an educator who knew quite a bit about the subject but was not able to break it down into meaningful chunks so that it was comprehensible.

Competence is further enhanced by practices related to teacher clarity. When students understand the alignment between the learning intentions, the success criteria, and the tasks and assignments they complete, comprehension goes up. Students also benefit when they are provided with different examples and non-examples to further develop their understanding. In other words, the teacher doesn't just repeat the same lesson for those students who need reteaching.

> When students understand the alignment between the learning intentions, the success criteria, and the tasks and assignments they complete, comprehension goes up.

DYNAMISM

Dynamism is the degree of enthusiasm displayed for the classroom learning community and content being taught. It's the aspect of teacher credibility that educators activate in order to motivate students and make the learning relevant. Dynamism also involves the educator's ability to pique students' curiosity when perhaps the subject might otherwise be considered dry or dull. Dynamic educators find ways to make learning interesting and useful while conveying that the students they are teaching are valued and appreciated.

IMMEDIACY

The final dimension of teacher credibility is immediacy, which refers to how accessible and relatable students feel their teacher is. Students notice if teachers favor particular students or if every learner is a valued member of the classroom learning community. While teachers need to be accessible, immediacy also means that there's a sense of urgency within the classroom. The point that is communicated by teachers with a strong sense of immediacy is that students' learning time and classwork are important and purposeful; their time is not to be wasted.

Consider your own teaching, either in the past with PK–12 students or now with adults. How did you—or do you—maintain your credibility? Which of the four factors are strengths of yours? Which would you like to develop further?

COLLECTIVE TEACHER EFFICACY: FOUR CONDITIONS THAT LEAVE LASTING IMPRESSIONS ON GROUPS OF STUDENTS AND EDUCATORS

Teachers must perceive that, as a team and a school, they have the wherewithal to positively impact student learning.

Collective teacher efficacy (CTE) is one of the top influences on student learning, with an effect size of 1.36 (Visible Learning Meta[X], 2021, www.visiblelearningmetax .com). Simply said, it has one of the highest degrees of potential to accelerate learning. That said, many educators confuse efficacy with activity; they mistakenly believe that sharing lesson plans or meeting together will create collective teacher efficacy, which will then somehow result in greater student achievement. Rather, for CTE to emerge, the group must have evidence to draw from. Teachers must perceive that, as a team and a school, they have the wherewithal to positively impact student learning. Importantly, CTE occurs when there is a shared belief that teachers across the school are working collaboratively toward challenging goals; CTE doesn't emerge when working alone.

As Bandura (1993) noted, efficacy is more likely to occur when four specific conditions are fostered:

- Mastery experiences
- Vicarious learning
- Social persuasion
- Regulation of affective states

Each of these can be fostered through team interactions, so let's look at each aspect more closely now.

MASTERY EXPERIENCES

By far the strongest of the four factors, mastery experiences are past successes. When you have been effective previously, it increases your belief that you can replicate that success. As one general example, the collective efficacy of a sports team is enhanced with game wins, which serve as fuel for future wins. In the work of PLC+ teams, a mastery experience can occur when the team collaboratively identifies a need, develops a plan to address the need, implements the plan, gathers evidence of impact, and reflects upon it. This way of working together is much more focused than meeting on Tuesdays to share lesson plans with each other, and when this mastery occurs, teams are empowered and motivated to continue learning with and from each other.

PAUSE AND PONDER

Identify some experiences that have built your belief in a team. How did mastery figure into that experience? What experiences do you plan for teachers to ensure that they experience mastery, both collectively and individually?

VICARIOUS LEARNING

Vicarious learning occurs when we're not directly part of the team, but we see and feel their success and say, "We can do that, too." Vicarious learning is contagious in schools if we allow it to be. When teams are empowered to share details about their own learning because they have evidence of impact, it has a ripple effect on everyone. Regular opportunities to learn across teams are vital to the progress of the schoolwide professional learning community.

Vicarious learning is contagious in schools if we allow it to be.

SOCIAL PERSUASION

Social persuasion occurs when educators are reinforced by an authority figure or someone they admire. Social persuasion is less effective than mastery and vicarious learning, but it can often be an entry point for some educators and teams. The encouragement you and others provide is another important lever in raising the efficacy of teams.

REGULATION OF AFFECTIVE STATES

The emotional tenor of the team—or the culture—is what is meant by affective states. Teams that build deep trust and psychological safety for all members engage in dialogue where assumptions about students, their abilities, and their rates of learning are challenged. Statements such as "They can't read at grade level" and "We've always done it this way" are rarely heard when these teams meet. Instead, teams with positive, learning-focused cultures can discuss and challenge each other's thinking without shredding relationships.

PAUSE AND PONDER

How can you foster the four aspects of collective efficacy? What actions can you take to ensure that teacher teams regularly are engaged in activities that promote mastery experiences, vicarious experiences, social persuasion, and monitoring their affective states?

COMBINING FORCES: TEACHER CREDIBILITY AND COLLECTIVE TEACHER EFFICACY

PLC+ teams work to further both teacher credibility and collective teacher efficacy; students benefit from both. Teacher credibility makes a significant difference in the lives of students in individual classrooms. Collective teacher efficacy is even more powerful because there's a shared belief that the educators in this school are working together to meet the academic, social, and emotional needs of every student. There's an understanding that an individual educator cannot be all things to every student, but by working together, we are more likely to positively impact each of our learners.

There is an interplay between teachers' credibility with students and their efficacy as a member of a team (see Figure 8.1). We have named each of the quadrants to help us determine support plans for each situation. Note that there are valid reasons that teachers are in each of these various quadrants. Additionally, these categories are situational, not static. A teacher may be in one quadrant when placed in a group with certain people but in another quadrant with a different team.

> PLC+ teams work to further both teacher credibility and collective teacher efficacy; students benefit from both.

FIGURE 8.1

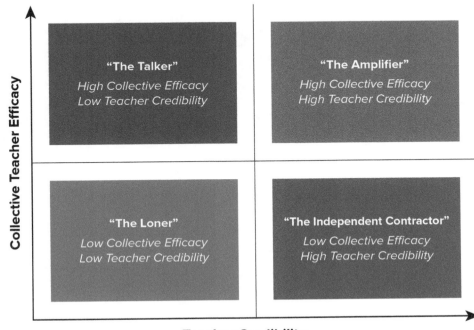

Source: Adapted from Fisher, Frey, and Smith (2020, p. 27).

The characteristics and actions of each of these roles are presented in Figure 8.2. Again, we don't want to suggest that teachers fit exclusively into one of these categories, or that individuals possess all of the characteristics in a particular category. Rather, we present it as a way of thinking about how to support the unique needs of teams and their members.

FIGURE 8.2

CHARACTERISTICS OF FOUR TYPES OF EDUCATORS

Collective Teacher Efficacy (vertical axis)

The Talker
- Professionally generous with colleagues
- Values the company of colleagues
- Holds an optimistic view of colleagues and the school
- Likes working with adults; tolerates students
- Rarely turns ideas into action or has impact
- Holds a pessimistic view of students and has low expectations for them
- Held in low regard by students

The Amplifier
- Professionally generous with colleagues
- Seeks to learn shoulder-to-shoulder with colleagues
- Has an optimistic view of students, colleagues, and the school
- Perceived by students as competent, trustworthy, dynamic, and caring
- Perceived by colleagues as competent, trustworthy, dynamic, and accessible
- Students and colleagues reach their potential because of this person

The Loner
- Is isolated socially and emotionally by colleagues
- Practice is private and not shared
- Colleagues avoid engaging beyond necessary interactions
- Holds a pessimistic view of students, colleagues, and the school
- Students are wary and avoid interacting beyond minimal compliance
- Not held in high regard by students
- Wonders whether this is the right profession for them

The Independent Contractor
- Isolates self socially and emotionally from colleagues
- Practice is private, secretive, and not shared
- Has an optimistic view of students
- Has a pessimistic view of colleagues and the school
- Is not open to the ideas of others
- Perceived by students as competent, trustworthy, dynamic, and accessible

Teacher Credibility (horizontal axis)

Source: Adapted from Fisher, Frey, and Smith (2020, p. 27).

SELF-ASSESSMENT

The leader's goal is to support every educator to become an amplifier. The amplifier is an educator who is professionally generous with colleagues. This person holds an optimistic view of students, colleagues, and the school. The amplifier possesses a learning disposition; they are not perceived as a know-it-all. Because of their high levels of credibility, the amplifier helps students and adults to reach their potential. However, these are potentially people that are ready to become activators on their PLC+ teams. What are some specific actions you might take to develop the qualities of an amplifier? We've listed a few ways to get you started; please use the extra bullets in each quadrant to note additional ideas.

THE TALKER

- Encourage action to accompany ideas
- Partner with the independent contractor or amplifier
- Build credibility with students:
  - Trust
  - Competence
  - Dynamism
  - Immediacy
- Ask for their input
-
-
-

THE AMPLIFIER

- Recognize their efforts and strengths
- Check in weekly to make sure they don't burn out
- Ask for their input
-
-
-
-
-

THE LONER

- Find out why there is a disconnect between this person and students and colleagues
- Identify at least one strength
- Give a role on the PLC+ team
- Make this person a priority for weekly check-ins
- Build credibility with colleagues
  - Trust
  - Competence
  - Dynamism
  - Immediacy
- Build credibility with students
  - Trust
  - Competence
  - Dynamism
  - Immediacy
- Ask for their input
-
-
-
-

THE INDEPENDENT CONTRACTOR

- Find out why they're disconnected from colleagues
- Elicit their input about expertise to share with their team
- Encourage this person to allow colleagues to observe and learn
- Build credibility with colleagues
  - Trust
  - Competence
  - Dynamism
  - Immediacy
- Ask for their input
-
-
-
-
-

Visit the companion website at
resources.corwin.com/PLC+forleaders
for downloadable resources.

NOTES

Idea 9

THERE'S MORE THAN ONE WAY TO FORM PLC+ TEAMS.

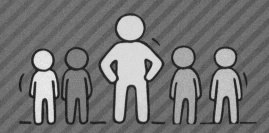

Essential Question: How should teacher teams be formed to ensure that adult learning is facilitated such that student learning is enhanced?

Traditionally, PLC teams are composed of teachers at a single grade level or content area. However, these configurations, while sometimes effective, are not the only ways to organize teams of educators to accomplish the common challenge. As we noted earlier in this companion guide, there are several problems that arise when teams are limited to people who teach the same thing. These include the following:

- Finding common planning time

- Having different needs and goals

- Forcing people to work together

To get the most out of collaboration time, strategic leaders consider alternate and flexible team formations that can maximize teaching and learning.

Adults are more likely to learn when they have a voice and choice in types of learning experiences, can draw upon those experiences, and perceive the learning as being useful to them (Knowles et al., 2012). Yet too often teams are created without regard to educators' interests, needs, and preferences. Grade-level or department-based teams can be a false limiter, meaning that other configurations may be more effective.

Of course, some common challenges lend themselves to grade-level configuration. Schools have teachers with various amounts of experience who want professional learning that's relevant to their own classroom and learning needs. But when educators feel obligated to be part of a team that doesn't meet their adult learning needs, there is often less impact and less collaboration—and, as a result, less student learning.

PAUSE AND PONDER

Consider the teams you've been on. What made them effective? How did the team decide what to focus on? Could there have been more effective ways to organize the team's work?

TYPES OF PLC TEAM CONFIGURATIONS

Grade-level or department configurations are the most common way that PLC+ teams are formed. When this is the case, it is important to regularly assess how teams are composed because there may be new teachers to the profession, new teachers to the team, or auxiliary personnel such as counselors, special education teachers, intervention specialists, and others who serve in multiple capacities. Don't make the mistake of leaving the team formation to chance. The second-grade team is likely to be quite different from the third-grade team. Instructional leaders must also monitor and support meeting structures because scheduling issues and other commitments may impede the team's collaboration time.

In some cases, there's not a designated team for the singletons, which can block the flow of information, instruction, and other communication. Since we don't want anyone to be lost in the shuffle, instructional leaders must regularly oversee how teams are functioning and determine if any supports or reconfigurations are needed. It's okay to reconfigure if it's not working.

A second way that teams can form is by interest in a common challenge. When you invite educators to self-select an interest-based team, they are more likely to find PLC time engaging and valuable. Further, when teachers have choice in the team and in the learning experience, they are more likely to internalize professional learning and transfer it into their repertoire. As we discussed in Idea 7, the principles of adult learning include the following (Knowles et al., 2012):

> Instructional leaders must regularly oversee how teams are functioning and determine if any supports or reconfigurations are needed.

- Self-direction

- Transformation

- Experience

- Mentorship

- Mental orientation

- Motivation

- Readiness to learn

These principles are frequently violated when educators are forced into groups (eliminating motivation) or are assigned topics that they are not interested in (eliminating self-direction). Given that schools are multigenerational workplaces, it's important to recognize that different generations expect more—or less—self-direction (see Figure 9.1).

FIGURE 9.1

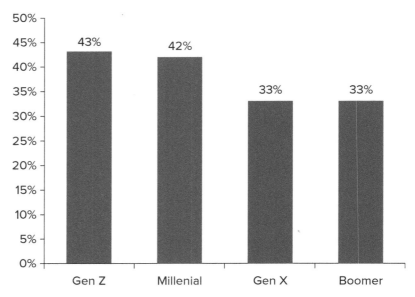

LEARNERS WHO PREFER SELF-DIRECTED AND INDEPENDENT LEARNING BY GENERATION

Source: Adapted from Censuswide (2019).

PAUSE AND PONDER

Consider the generations of educators at your school or district. How are the PLC and the teams that operate within the PLC impacted by a multigenerational workplace?

Self-selecting teams can be accomplished in various ways, including a survey in which educators nominate topics. The instructional leader who uses a tight-loose-tight approach is an active part of the self-selection process, ensuring that the topics are relevant, worthy, and aligned with the vision and needs of the school.

Teams should have at least three educators; we believe eight should be the maximum to maintain voice and accountability. Teams and the interests they select typically meet over six to nine weeks, which means there's a starting and an ending point for each team. Throughout one school year, an educator could potentially be on four sequential teams, giving that teacher multiple opportunities to engage with—and learn from—other educators they may not normally encounter or interact with in their grade level or department.

For example, teachers at Marvilla Middle School used a self-selected configuration of those from different grade levels and subjects who were interested in improving oral language development for multilingual students. This became a great experience for Ms. Jackson, a new teacher with limited experience who wanted to learn how to integrate appropriate scaffolds for multilingual learners. By pairing with more veteran team members, Ms. Jackson learned strategies from experienced peers and was able to implement them immediately. Furthermore, since this was an interest-based PLC+ team, everyone had the same goal: to improve students' oral language development and collect evidence of learning in order to determine the effectiveness of their instruction. Ms. Jackson was more comfortable asking for and getting assistance as she and her teacher colleagues engaged in collaborative professional learning.

A third way to configure teams is vertically. In this situation, there may be educators from different grade levels or departments who collaborate on a common skill, noting the nuances of the skill and how it is developed over time. Additionally, this configuration provides the team with opportunities to examine how the skill becomes more complex as students ascend the grade levels.

As you form vertical groups, make sure the grade bands for the PLC+ teams are practical. For instance, a kindergarten teacher, second-grade teacher, and sixth-grade teacher may not be the best configuration given the gaps in grade levels represented. Instead, the instructional leader can identify the grade bands (e.g., grades 3, 4, and 5) and perhaps allow teachers to choose a particular standard or skill. This follows our tight-loose-tight approach because the instructional leader is involved when a team unites around a common challenge. The configuration of teams and expected learning outcomes are tight; how teams choose to reach those outcomes is loose.

Given that there are both gaps and redundancies in standards, how might the addition of vertical teams help address these issues? What impact could nontraditional PLC+ team membership have on examining and addressing expectations for rigor in the school or district?

Forming teams is a critical leadership action that should not be left to chance when there are better options that further student learning, educator morale, and team learning. A tight-loose-tight approach supports each of these facets. There is a range of benefits that occur when teams are formed with intention and purpose. Educators—ourselves included—feel more productive, impactful, and joyful when there are opportunities to be innovative. Further, the motivation to learn from others is enhanced by the knowledge that these teams aren't permanent. In addition, when we offer a range of group options to educators, the costs of attending professional development events and conferences are reduced while internal capacity is strengthened. When schools capitalize on their own knowledge and skills, teachers are empowered. Funds traditionally earmarked for isolated professional development events could be reallocated more purposefully.

PAUSE AND PONDER

Take a few moments to note the PLC+ team configurations at your site. Which teams are working? Why? Are there teams where people feel stuck? Might there be opportunities to reconfigure your PLC+ teams? Consulting with your staff about options will help ensure they feel included and invested in their professional learning. List some ideas you would like to explore with them further.

LEARNING FROM OTHER ORGANIZATIONS

As we consider our options for creating and supporting teams, we can also learn from examples found in other industries, such as business, health care, government, and nonprofit. Page (n.d.) notes that there are six important aspects to consider when forming teams (see Figure 9.2).

FIGURE 9.2

BUILDING AN EFFECTIVE TEAM

1. **Define the purpose.** What is the reason that the team has been formed? What should the team accomplish as a result of interacting? Does the team have a mission and vision for their work, and does each person know how they contribute to the work of the team?

2. **Assemble the team.** Select individuals who can collaborate and support one another, while also pushing the thinking of one another. Team members should have skills that complement one another, and teams should have a range of perspectives.

3. **Determine the goals.** Identify the goals that the team should address. In PLC+, we call this the common challenge and have developed several protocols for teams to identify their goals. The team may need to develop a schedule or timeline to keep them focused on the goals.

4. **Set expectations.** Clear roles and responsibilities are important for team members to feel productive and contribute to the group. Often, these are expressed as the norms for the group. It's also useful to address how conflicts are addressed before the team actually has a conflict.

5. **Monitor and review.** Develop systems to monitor the success of the team, including how members are interacting and the impact that they have. Leaders can observe the team at work and talk with individual members to determine what is, and is not, working.

6. **Celebrate and reward.** Success is a powerful motivator. Make sure that teams take time to recognize their successes and pause to celebrate them. There are any number of ways to celebrate success, but recognize that these celebrations serve to motivate team members and build their individual and collective efficacy.

Source: Adapted from Page (n.d.).

SELF-ASSESSMENT

Using the six factors outlined in Figure 9.2, analyze your teams using the following scale, with 1 being very much in need to 5 being strongly evident. Which of these six factors are strong and which need attention?

FACTOR	RATIONALE FOR RATING	IDEAS FOR IMPROVEMENT
1. Define the purpose. 1 · · · 2 · · · 3 · · · 4 · · · 5		
2. Assemble the team. 1 · · · 2 · · · 3 · · · 4 · · · 5		
3. Determine the goals. 1 · · · 2 · · · 3 · · · 4 · · · 5		
4. Set expectations. 1 · · · 2 · · · 3 · · · 4 · · · 5		
5. Monitor and review. 1 · · · 2 · · · 3 · · · 4 · · · 5		
6. Celebrate and reward. 1 · · · 2 · · · 3 · · · 4 · · · 5		

online resources

Visit the companion website at
resources.corwin.com/PLC+forleaders
for downloadable resources.

NOTES

Idea 10

LEADERS NEED TO IDENTIFY TRENDS AND DEVELOP PLANS TO SUPPORT EDUCATORS AS THEY WORK TOGETHER.

Essential Question: What patterns am I noticing in different teams, and what actions should the leadership team and I take to support teacher learning?

Focusing on instructional improvement can be overwhelming for leaders, especially given the range of other tasks they must accomplish each day. Between supervising lunch periods, communicating with parents, responding to emails, and managing resources, there often is not a lot of time left to focus on instructional quality. But it's hard to improve the instructional program if the leaders are rarely observing the work of teacher teams or classroom instruction in real time. As Robinson et al. (2008) noted in their meta-analysis on instructional leadership, "The closer educational leaders get to the core business of teaching and learning, the more likely they are to have a positive impact on students' outcomes" (p. 664).

Having said that, spending time in classrooms is not going to improve student outcomes if you do not use the data to make decisions. In many key ways, leaders can follow the same approach that effective teachers take to lead their students forward. Effective teachers collect and analyze evidence to decide where student learning should go next. They use this evidence to provide individual feedback to students—and on a broader scale, they use it to identify trends and make decisions about what to focus on with the whole class, when to strategically group students, and when to provide individualized instruction, support, and intervention. Similarly, effective leaders should collect and analyze evidence to identify trends and make informed decisions about where teachers and teams should go next, how PLC+ teams should be grouped, and what additional support teams may need.

How do you see a connection between teachers using evidence formatively to make decisions and leaders using evidence to make decisions? Why do most leaders focus on individual feedback to teachers rather than noticing trends and taking action with groups of educators?

LEVELED DECISION MAKING

Before we share ways to collect and analyze team trend data, we want to focus on ways you can make decisions with staff members and communicate about those selections. It almost goes without saying, but leaders must communicate clearly. This communication competence comes from leaders seeking to determine what is understood, recognizing that what leaders or others say is not always what individuals hear. Far too often there are communication and consensus gaps in schools because of the lack of understanding related to the types of decisions that are being made.

One effective method for leaders to better ensure that how they communicate builds relationships and establishes consensus is an approach called *leveled decision making.* Using this method, leaders share upfront the types of decisions that are being made and how input from others will be considered and/or acted upon. In this section, we will briefly focus on three different levels of decisions.

> *Level 1 decisions* are "tight" decisions leaders make around issues involving safety, legality, and morality. These decisions will not be voted on, and input will not be sought. Leaders with communication competence share with staff that they are not going to waste their time by seeking input on these level 1 decisions because they are simply not up for debate.

> Leaders should make level 1 decisions to bar any actions and practices in schools and classrooms that have been shown to drastically decrease the probability that learning will occur. For example, we mentioned earlier that round-robin reading has been shown time and time again to be an ineffective and even detrimental method toward students' literacy development (Ash et al., 2009). It is more than fair for a leader to say, "Round-robin reading is a practice that is off-limits in our classrooms." Why? Because it's an academic safety issue: it harms student learning. Such a pronouncement would be a level 1 decision.

> *Level 2 decisions* involve issues that are very important to the school moving forward and that will have a direct impact on teacher and team actions where the leader wants and seeks input from staff. This is a loosening of the decision making. In these cases, leaders possess 51% of the vote, but they truly value and consider teacher and team input in order to make the best possible decision for the school community. Here, too, leaders communicate clearly upfront (tight). In a level 2 decision, not everyone will get what they want, but they are consulted. For a variety of reasons, it's possible the leader may still need to change direction or more tightly shape the path and actions of teachers and teams.

> *Level 3 decisions* involve issues where the majority rules. This is an example of a loose approach. Leaders ensure that the options and possibilities are laid out so everyone is aware of the options, feels heard, and recognizes that all voices and votes are equal.

The power here is not simply in the process of making leveled decisions—it is in the clear communication to teachers and teams up front prior to seeking input about the degree to which that could influence or determine decisions. Figure 10.1 contains more sample decisions at levels 1, 2, and 3.

FIGURE 10.1

LEVELS OF DECISION MAKING

LEVEL OF DECISION	PRIMARILY USED FOR DECISIONS RELATED TO . . .	LEADER ACTIONS/ INPUT SOUGHT	EXAMPLES
1	Safety, legality, morality	None; decisions are shared with staff and teams, but not in a manner that seeks input, feedback, or consensus	• Anything related to the physical safety of all staff and students • Legality, such as implementation of practices related to the Individuals with Disabilities Education Act (IDEA), special education, etc. • Actions that are proven to be related to increasing the probability of learning, such as the use of evidence-based instructional practices, adherence to content standards
2	Expected adult actions related to school, PLC+ team, and classroom actions	Creates guidelines for staff and teams for input on how they will reach expected outcomes Shares that all ideas from staff and teams will be considered but that the leader (or perhaps the leadership team) has veto power	• The specific common challenges teams commit and work on • How teams establish and share clarity with students • How teams decide on and implement effective evidence-based instructional actions
3	Actions and decisions that will not negatively impact learning, relationship, or culture regardless of what is decided upon	Shares options for possible decisions on the table and explains that majority "voting" or input received will be the deciding factor for moving forward	• When PLC+ teams meet (once a minimum amount of time to meet and actions expected have been established) • The specific topic or focus for microteaching • When teams engage in learning walks (once a minimum expectation of when and what has been established)

What is the current reality of decision making in your school or district? How do you communicate your decision-making process as well as how input is considered and/or acted upon? In what ways could leveled decision making increase the communication competence of the leaders in your school or district?

EXPLORING DATA FOR TRENDS

East Middle School has been working on ensuring there is clarity present in all classrooms as a driver of both effective instruction and assessment. They believe passionately that students should be able to articulate what they are learning, how they will know when they are successful, and what their next learning step(s) will be. Teachers have engaged in professional learning related to teacher clarity and know that this was a level 1 decision.

The leaders have allowed the PLC+ teams to make their own decisions on how they will go about working together and implementing clarity in their classrooms. Notice the tight-loose structure? Now the leaders also need to consider adding tight to the process.

The principal, John Whipkey, and his leadership team conduct a series of learning walks and monitor three data points:

1. The presence and accessibility of learning intentions and success criteria in the classroom

2. The alignment of the lesson to the success criteria

3. The students' ability to authentically articulate what they are learning and how they will be successful

They collect the following data:

GRADES 6, 7, AND 8	LEARNING INTENTIONS AND SUCCESS CRITERIA PRESENT AND ACCESSIBLE	LESSON ALIGNED TO LEARNING INTENTIONS AND SUCCESS CRITERIA
September Number of classrooms visited (43)	38 classrooms	15 classrooms
October Number of classrooms visited (42)	40 classrooms	17 classrooms

The leaders provide the following student voice rubric to all staff to help determine the level of clarity perceived by students. They understand that adults do not get to determine if they are teaching with clarity; the students do.

	NEEDS ATTENTION (NA)	DEVELOPING (D)	IMPLEMENTED (I)
Question: What are you learning today?	The student is unable to articulate what they are learning or can only reference a task or activity.	The student articulates what they are learning (articulates the target/learning intention).	The student articulates what they are learning and how this connects to the learning task or activity.
Question: How will you know you've learned it/know you are successful?	The student is unable to articulate how they will know they have learned the target or gives no response.	The student articulates how they will know they have learned the target *by referring to the success criteria.*	The student refers to the success criteria and can articulate how the success criteria link to their current learning task.

During the learning walks, the leaders ask various students two questions: *What are you learning today?* and *How will you know when you will be successful?* The following data are compiled.

MONTH (NUMBER OF STUDENTS SURVEYED IN PARENTHESES)	WHAT ARE YOU LEARNING TODAY?	HOW WILL YOU KNOW YOU'VE LEARNED IT/ KNOW YOU ARE SUCCESSFUL?
September (162)	NA: 84 (52%) D: 50 (31%) I: 28 (17%)	NA: 99 (61%) D: 51 (31%) I: 12 (7%)
October (151)	NA: 68 (45%) D: 40 (26%) I: 43 (28%)	NA: 76 (50%) D: 57 (38%) I: 18 (12%)

NA: Not apparent; D: Developing; I: Implemented

Numbers are rounded to the nearest full percentage. Totals are not always 100%.

The data provides the leadership team at East Middle School with a picture of what is happening (and not happening) in relation to the clarity focus during PLC+ meetings and what is being transferred into classroom practice. Yes, it is obvious from the data that teams have developed learning intentions and success criteria. What is also clear, however, is a lack of alignment between the lesson and expected clarity because students are unable to articulate what they are learning and how they will know when they are successful.

This leads the leadership team to suggest a common challenge for teams to consider as well as to identify additional professional learning and coaching opportunities that can be provided. Rather than spending significant amounts of time providing individual teachers with feedback, the leadership team decides to address this as a systems issue because the data indicates that most students lack clarity. The common challenge for the school's next PLC+ cycle: *Students do not consistently understand what they are learning and how they will know they are successful, reducing the likelihood they will master the learning.*

NOTES

PAUSE AND PONDER

Looking at the data from East Middle School, what other actions might you recommend to them? What strengths did you notice that they could build on? What additional learning might their teams need?

TEAM TREND DATA

The example from East Middle School focuses on a level 1 decision. But sometimes teams are in very different places, and the leaders' response is not as simple as taking action with the whole staff. In these cases, leaders may need to provide individual feedback to teachers as well as feedback to the team as a whole. In addition, thoughtful leaders can also mobilize resources on their campus, or within their school system, to support the change that is needed, based on the evidence presented.

For example, the leadership team at Baristo Canyon High School observes teams as they interact, and they visit classrooms to observe implementation. One team focuses on academic vocabulary and consists of four teachers (two science, one history, and one career/technical education teacher). Their common challenge is students' use of academic vocabulary in speaking and writing. The leaders note that the team possesses strengths and has implemented some of the ideas that have come from their collaboration. However, these teachers are not strong when it comes to direct instruction of words or selecting words with multiple meanings (see Figure 10.2).

As a team, they note which teachers need feedback about a specific aspect of their lessons versus when a teacher needs coaching. The difference between these two is this:

- *Feedback* is oriented to past performance. It is useful after observing a lesson or a team meeting. The feedback is about evidence of what was, or was not, accomplished.

- *Coaching* is about future performance. It is necessary for applying feedback to future lessons or team meetings. Coaching includes direction giving coupled with resources and supports.

Sometimes the leaders identify that a level 1 decision has been violated, and then the focus of the conversation is on corrective actions. In this case, the school has agreed to significantly reduce worksheets and have students engage in note taking and graphic organizers, which is not how the team always proceeds. However, one teacher, Tanya, has continued to use lots of worksheets to fill out. That calls for corrective action with her, but not with the entire team.

Note in this plan (see Figure 10.2) that there is also a focus on the team and how leaders can leverage the team to accomplish specific things. In doing so, the leadership team can save time because they are not focused on doing everything individually, nor are they wasting the time of other teachers at the school who do not need this information. Further, the leadership team notes what they can do with the leader of the teacher team to support deeper implementation. Finally, they note the ways in which they can mobilize site and central office resources to support this team and their continued development.

NOTES

_____

_____

_____

_____

_____

_____

_____

_____

_____

_____

_____

FIGURE 10.2

ACTION PLANNING WITH TEAMS

Name of Team or Team Members: Academic Vocabulary Team

TREND DATA FROM NOVEMBER-DECEMBER OBSERVATIONS

Strengths	Challenges	Priorities
• Word solving of vocab • Agreed upon Tier 3 words • Used in writing tasks • Used in collaboration	• No focus on Tier 2 • Limited direct instruction	Identify Tier 2 words for instruction and add direct instruction to plans

INDIVIDUAL TEACHER SUPPORT

1. **Name and Date** Raphael	[x] Feedback Lesson on word solving [ ] Coaching [ ] Corrective action	**Notes/Follow-Up Date**
2. **Name and Date** Leeza	[ ] Feedback [x] Coaching Increase implementation of collaborative tasks [ ] Corrective action	**Notes/Follow-Up Date**
3. **Name and Date** Sonia	[x] Feedback Lesson on word solving [ ] Coaching [ ] Corrective action	**Notes/Follow-Up Date**
4. **Name and Date** Tanya	[ ] Feedback [ ] Coaching [x] Corrective action Only saw worksheets	**Notes/Follow-Up Date**

TEAM SUPPORT

Immediately	Within 30 Days	Within 60 Days
[x] Professional learning on selecting Tier 2 words	[x] Professional learning on direct instruction	[ ] Professional learning on _____
[x] Team meeting	[ ] Team meeting	[ ] Team meeting
[ ] Learning walk	[ ] Learning walk	[x] Learning walk
[ ] Collaboration protocol	[x] Collaboration protocol	[ ] Collaboration protocol
[ ]	[ ]	[ ]

TEAM LEADER SUPPORT

	Notes
[ ] Facilitation skills training	The team agreed to implement collaborative tasks, but two of the classrooms did not include collaboration
[ ] Protocol training	
[ ] Data discussion training	
[x] Review team agreements	

ON-SITE RESOURCES

People, programs, or initiatives you can mobilize to support this priority	Actions these individuals should take or how you can access programs or initiatives
• Coach • Vice Principal	COACH: Design professional learning on selecting Tier 2 words; design PL on direct instruction; support team lead with implementation of collaboration VP: Visit classrooms for implementation of collaboration

CENTRAL OFFICE RESOURCES

People, programs, or initiatives you can mobilize to support this priority	Actions these individuals should take or how you can access programs or initiatives
• Sample lessons	Use the sample lessons on direct instruction as examples for teachers to review and observe

Looking at the data from the team at Baristo Canyon High School, what other actions might you recommend based on the data? What strengths did you notice that they could build on with their team? What additional learning might their teams need?

SELF-ASSESSMENT

Choose a team to study at your site. Visit their PLC+ team meetings and observe classroom instruction. Then complete the following action planning with the team trends tool below. Identify the trends, in terms of strengths and challenges, and select a priority based on the data. Consider each member of the team and the team as a whole. Decide what you can accomplish with the team immediately and over the next few months. Finally, identify resources that you can use to support the team, as well as more specialized supports for individuals with greater needs. After all, schools have many teams, and each of them needs attention to cultivate their growth.

ACTION PLANNING WITH TEAMS

Name of Team or Team Members:

TREND DATA		
Strengths	**Challenges**	**Priorities**
•	•	

INDIVIDUAL TEACHER SUPPORT		
1. Name and Date	[ ] Feedback [ ] Coaching [ ] Corrective action	**Notes/Follow-Up Date**
2. Name and Date	[ ] Feedback [ ] Coaching [ ] Corrective action	**Notes/Follow-Up Date**
3. Name and Date	[ ] Feedback [ ] Coaching [ ] Corrective action	**Notes/Follow-Up Date**
4. Name and Date	[ ] Feedback [ ] Coaching [ ] Corrective action	**Notes/Follow-Up Date**

(Continued)

(Continued)

TEAM SUPPORT

Immediately	Within 30 Days	Within 60 Days
[ ] Professional learning on _____	[ ] Professional learning on _____	[ ] Professional learning on _____
[ ] Team meeting	[ ] Team meeting	[ ] Team meeting
[ ] Learning walk	[ ] Learning walk	[ ] Learning walk
[ ] Collaboration protocol	[ ] Collaboration protocol	[ ] Collaboration protocol
[ ]	[ ]	[ ]

TEAM LEADER SUPPORT

[ ] Facilitation skills training	**Notes**
[ ] Protocol training	
[ ] Data discussion training	
[ ]	

ON-SITE RESOURCES

People, programs, or initiatives you can mobilize to support this priority	Actions these individuals should take or how you can access programs or initiatives
•	

CENTRAL OFFICE RESOURCES

People, programs, or initiatives you can mobilize to support this priority	Actions these individuals should take or how you can access programs or initiatives
•	

Visit the companion website at
resources.corwin.com/PLC+forleaders
for downloadable resources.

Idea 11

ACTIVATORS ARE CRUCIAL TO HELPING ENSURE THE LEARNING OF ALL ADULTS IN PLC+ SETTINGS.

Essential Question: How are you currently supporting and developing activators as drivers of learning within your PLC+ structure?

One aspect that sets PLC+ apart from previous models is our belief that the learning of the adults is paramount for the success of the professional learning community. A cross-cutting value in the framework is *activation*. Those who guide the overall functioning of the PLC+ team are activators because they "add ideas, ask questions, notice nonverbal cues, and help the team make decisions" (Fisher et al., 2019b). This activation comes from within the group, not externally. Crucially, they are full members of the team, not administrators or instructional coaches who serve a single role as a facilitator but who do not engage in the work.

Activators are also the catalyst that sparks the PLC+ team and ensures that the learning of the adults is always moving forward. But we mustn't assume activators are only those in the more vocal roles. For example, someone who takes copious notes and ensures that agendas are sent out and that the PLC+ team meetings are always organized is also activating. Ideally, over time, every teacher possesses the skills and dispositions to contribute to the activation of the PLC+ team.

With this in mind, we suggest that leaders who are initially engaging in the PLC+ process carefully build a cadre of core activators within each PLC+ team. Core activators are the team members you have identified as being on the leading edge of moving their teams to action. The people you have previously identified as being amplifiers may also be predisposed to serve as core activators (see

Idea 8 for more information on amplifiers). There are three actions leaders should take to support these core activators to drive activation skills across the entire team:

- Determining core activators for PLC+ teams

- Ensuring core activators can support the school or district's professional learning

- Having support structures in place for core activators

We will discuss each of these actions in more detail next.

DETERMINING CORE ACTIVATORS FOR PLC+ TEAMS

As you determine who will serve in the core role of activating and leading the team, we propose that you consider the five critical qualities of an activator (the 5 Cs): *clarity, consciousness, competence, confidence,* and *credibility.* Identify teachers you believe possess these qualities (see Figure 11.1).

NOTES

_____

_____

_____

_____

_____

_____

_____

_____

_____

_____

_____

_____

_____

FIGURE 11.1

FIVE CRITICAL QUALITIES OF ACTIVATORS

QUALITIES	DESCRIPTION	TEACHERS WHO POSSESS THIS QUALITY
Clarity	Help set and communicate team direction in both the short and long term	
Consciousness	Possess strong levels of social awareness when working with colleagues	
Competence	Have the ability to guide conversations (even when they are difficult)	
Confidence	Have a strong sense of self-efficacy and collective efficacy to overcome challenges to reach goals	
Credibility	Have earned the trust of colleagues; they have a record of under-promising and over-delivering	

Source: Adapted from Nagel et al. (2020, p. 28).

Consider your school's current makeup of staff. Are there adults who possess all five of these qualities? Are there adults who possess many of these qualities? How can you leverage the talents of these folks to be your core activators to best lead the learning of the adults on all PLC+ teams? Keep in mind that teams should be filled with multiple activators.

ENSURING ACTIVATORS CAN SUPPORT THE SCHOOL'S OR DISTRICT'S PROFESSIONAL LEARNING

Professional learning that occurs at the school or district level can either be enhanced or inhibited, depending on its alignment with the professional learning community. This alignment provides further opportunities for continued application, practice, and mastery of the concepts being taught in professional learning.

Core activators must be competent in leading and guiding the learning within the PLC+ of the school's current professional learning focus areas. The activator's efficacy plays a major factor in the choice of activities, the amount of effort expended, and how long team members will sustain effort in dealing with stressful situations (Bandura, 1977). Core activators must be able to support the team's learning and progress so that when team members inevitably get stuck and experience an implementation dip (Satir et al., 2006; see Idea 6), the activators can help the team press on, engage in productive struggle, and overcome the challenge.

An ongoing goal in the PLC+ framework is to continuously cultivate the skills of an ever-increasing number of staff members to function as activators. Importantly, they are not operating in the traditional role of a facilitator who is outside the membership of the team. Nor does there need to be a sole activator who serves in this role in perpetuity. Mature teams should have several activators, and as the common challenge changes, so do the activators. However, core activators can serve as the leading edge in your effort to develop and enhance a PLC+ framework in your school or district.

Core activators do not need to be experts in what the PLC+ team is exploring. However, activators do need to exhibit a willingness to learn shoulder-to-shoulder with fellow members.

As one example, if a school is deeply focusing on restorative practices to promote desired student behavior outcomes, then the core activators of their PLC+ teams cannot be individuals with little to no knowledge of how to implement practices in their own classrooms. Remember, as the common challenge changes, the people best able to serve as activators can change, too. See Figure 11.2 for an example of a principal's thinking about who might best be equipped to serve as activators for a common challenge about success criteria.

> An ongoing goal in the PLC+ framework is to continuously cultivate the skills of an ever-increasing number of staff to function as activators.

FIGURE 11.2

DETERMINING THE READINESS OF CORE ACTIVATORS TO LEAD PROFESSIONAL LEARNING ON PLC+ TEAMS

CURRENT PROFESSIONAL DEVELOPMENT FOCUS AREAS WITHIN YOUR SCHOOL OR DISTRICT	SUCCESS CRITERIA FOR IMPLEMENTATION	TEACHERS WHO HAVE EMBRACED THIS WORK AND CAN PROVIDE QUALITY EXAMPLES OF PRACTICES COMING TO LIFE IN THEIR CLASSROOMS/TEAMS	HOW CAN YOU CAPITALIZE ON THEIR KNOWLEDGE IN THE ROLE OF CORE ACTIVATORS?
Example: *The Success Criteria Playbook*	• Develop quality success criteria for all lessons. • Align lesson structure and assessment tools directly to success criteria. • Make success criteria accessible to all students. • Monitor student understanding of success criteria in terms of how they know what they are learning and when they will be successful.	Jane B. (Ninth-Grade ELA) Sam Y. (Biology) and Keisha R. (Physics) Marc A. (U.S. History) Bertha J. (Special Education) Steve S. (Grades 9–10 Transition) Kristen M. and Jacob Z. (Algebra, Geometry, Math Transition) Juan U. (Family and Consumer Science) Josey I. (Band/Choir)	All core subject areas have at least one or more teachers who have demonstrated successful implementation of *The Success Criteria Playbook*. As we examine our PLC+ team makeup and schedules, we will ensure they are in meetings that are designated specifically to support the growth and development of all our teachers and PLC+ teams.

HAVING SUPPORT STRUCTURES IN PLACE FOR CORE ACTIVATORS

Core activators are charged with contributing to the learning of their PLC+ teams as well as their own learning. Very often these individuals are classroom teachers with caseloads of students just like their peers. They have been given additional responsibilities, and with that—to some degree—have increased their existing workload. It's critical that leaders have built-in structures to support these individuals and to ensure first that we do not overburden them.

Without support structures in place, activators are at risk of feeling isolated. One method to support core activators is to set up structured and scheduled periodic debriefing opportunities for them to come together and share successes and challenges. This will also give them a chance to pool their collective knowledge and wisdom for how they are leading their PLC+ teams.

With that in mind, activators at your school may appreciate asynchronous opportunities, too. For instance, a Padlet or other collaborative digital bulletin board can be posted for activators to seek help from the activator community. Whether you opt for face-to-face communication or digital communication or a combination of both, be sure that activators also know how to protect confidentiality (i.e., ensuring that no names of individuals are used) and engage in discussion in ways that are humane and growth producing. See Figure 11.3 for examples of more support structures.

Schools that are in the initial stages of developing PLC+ processes, or expanding the number of activators at their site, should consider hosting book studies of *The PLC+ Activator's Guide* (Nagel et al., 2020). This resource offers activators methods for promoting the insights of the teacher team they belong to, as well as resolving common problems that emerge. Book studies are an excellent role for instructional coaches to lead and offer further support for activators.

FIGURE 11.3

ACTIVATOR DEBRIEF EXAMPLES

TYPE OF SUPPORT	EXAMPLE	WHEN
Core activator debriefings related to overcoming difficulties faced by PLC+ teams	Core activators bring topics related to addressing difficulties within the team. Activators brainstorm ideas for overcoming these challenges.	Second Thursday of the month
Core activator debriefings related to how PLC+ teams are navigating the school's current professional learning initiatives	Core activators bring evidence and ideas for how their PLC+ is growing in their professional learning.	Fourth Thursday of the month

NOTES

What structures are currently in place to support your activators? How successful have these structures been? What other opportunities can you provide core activators to share difficulties, successes, and the generation of solutions?

SELF-ASSESSMENT

The self-assessments in this companion playbook have been tools for you to apply to yourself as an instructional leader. However, we are supplying a different tool for this module. This one is to be taken by activators to inform you about the supports you design for them. It can be useful for you as a leader to survey core activators so that you can design supports for them; we provide a sample survey below. Once they have completed this survey, identify one or two areas to revise, and strengthen the supports they've requested.

SELF-ASSESSMENT FOR ACTIVATORS

Directions: I am seeking to identify areas of support for you as a core activator. Please reflect on a recent PLC+ team meeting. Can you provide an example of what worked or did not work? How do you rate your effectiveness (1 = ineffective; 2 = somewhat effective; 3 = mostly effective; 4 = very effective) in the situation? Your insights are valuable.

ESSENTIAL ACTIVATOR SKILLS AND ROUTINES	EVIDENCE OR EXAMPLE	HOW DO YOU RATE YOUR EFFECTIVENESS?			
Maintaining Focus on the Topic Identify specific instances when the team stayed focused.		1	2	3	4
Using Precise Language Note any times when the team focused on deep aspects of instruction and learning.		1	2	3	4
Mediating Conflict Describe when and how you helped the team to work through a difference of opinion.		1	2	3	4
Testing for Consensus Note any situations when the team arrived at consensus.		1	2	3	4
Intervening When Events Are Starting to Sidetrack From the Team Provide details as to how you helped reorient the group back to the question at hand.		1	2	3	4
Closing the Meeting Appropriately Reflect on the closure. Was the meeting summarized and were next steps agreed upon?		1	2	3	4

Source: Adapted from Nagel et al. (2020, p. 32).

Visit the companion website at
resources.corwin.com/PLC+forleaders
for downloadable resources.

NOTES

Idea 12

TEACHERS NEW TO THE PROFESSION OR NEW TO THE SCHOOL REQUIRE ATTENTION FOR THE PROFESSIONAL LEARNING COMMUNITY TO THRIVE.

Essential Question: How do we ensure that new teachers feel welcomed into the school and are acclimated to how adults learn together?

Welcoming a new teacher to a school and PLC+ team is an exciting time. Although instructional leaders play a critical role in a new teacher's first weeks and months, a broader team effort often ensures that their initial experiences are both positive and enriching. There are many benefits to developing an onboarding plan for teachers new to the profession or experienced teachers new to the school. This is especially true in an era where an increasing number of new teachers and alternatively certified teachers are being hired.

Specifically, there is evidence (Richter et al., 2022) that schools that provide systems of support and an onboarding approach for these teachers accomplish three crucial tasks:

1. Increased job satisfaction

2. Increased self-efficacy

3. Increased predictions that they will remain in the teaching field three years later

Whether or not novice teachers have had experience with student teaching in face-to-face learning environments, they will likely struggle to fully understand the needs and nuances of each student in their classroom. They will often need help to establish learning routines, along with curriculum and instructional expectations, and they may not have participated on a PLC+ team in the past. Understanding a new context is invaluable, as this process often sheds light on school culture, any unspoken rules that exist as tightly held traditions, and other expectations that would foster a smoother transition into the school.

Additionally, new teachers often want to blend in. They may be afraid to ask for help, or perhaps they don't know that they should ask for help. Onboarding processes can alleviate much of the anxieties that new teachers feel when they are hired for their first teaching assignment. Instructional leaders can anticipate and minimize some of those worries by investing in new teachers' transition to the school and their PLC+ team.

PAUSE AND PONDER

Who are the teachers new to the profession at your site? Are there teachers who are pursuing alternative licensure? Do you have experienced teachers who are new to the site? Inventory your staff and identify those who may need specialized supports.

ORIENTING TEACHERS TO THE PLC+ MODEL

Chances are very good that teachers who are new to the profession—whether licensed through conventional or alternative certification processes—are unfamiliar with how to work with adults in any formal way. As well, teachers who are new to the school or district, although not new to the profession, also have specialized needs as it relates to professional learning communities. Chances are good that they carry prior experience with the version of PLCs they have become familiar with in their previous assignment, and they may struggle to understand how PLC+ operates at your school.

TNTP, formerly known as The New Teachers Project, offers several suggestions for instructional leaders and PLC+ teams to consider when developing plans to onboard new teachers. Figure 12.1 presents a hierarchy of needs that can be prioritized and developed into orientation processes.

> Basic needs include not only the schedule for PLC+ team meetings but also further advice about time management.

FIGURE 12.1

A HIERARCHY OF NEEDS FOR NEW TEACHERS

Goals for PD, long-term aspirations, resources to meet goals — • **Professional Growth Plan**

Assessments, student achievement goals, common planning expectations — • **Academic Goals**

School mission and philosophy, team building, mentorship, coaching — • **Community**

Administrative expectations, student expectations, pacing guide, performance evaluation criteria — • **Expectations**

Bathroom, food, keys, ID, payroll, health insurance, supplies, dress code, class schedule — • **Basic Needs**

Next, we will use this model as a springboard for considering the unique considerations of onboarding teachers who are new to the PLC+ process.

> It's important that leaders and teams communicate guidelines in relation to the curriculum, instruction, and assessment of student learning.

BASIC NEEDS

As Maslow (1943) noted, the basic needs of new teachers form the foundation of whether other goals can be met. This is an ideal time for the instructional leader to determine the initial key ideas and information that the new teacher needs to know. When first hired, their basic needs include access to software systems, communication channels, and schedules. In addition, this should also include basic information about the PLC+ processes and procedures. Basic needs include not only the schedule for PLC+ team meetings but also further advice about time management. Novice teachers in particular may have other obligations concerning induction or university coursework for licensure. Meet with new teachers early to help them develop a yearlong calendar for school meetings and additional requirements that may conflict. No one likes to be unsure of schedules, and this allows for the new teacher and the team leader to resolve scheduling conflicts proactively.

PAUSE AND PONDER

What additional obligations exist for teachers who are new to the site?

EXPECTATIONS

Another consideration for instructional leaders and PLC+ teams is the expectations related to the instructional programs at the school. It's important that leaders and teams communicate guidelines in relation to the curriculum, instruction, and assessment of student learning.

The PLC+ process at your school or district also has shared agreements about the development of common challenges; team roles and responsibilities, including activators; and enabling conditions that allow teams to thrive. Teams are especially useful in being able to outline expectations and to reestablish shared agreements about the function and process the PLC+ team uses. Whether a teacher is new to the profession or new to the site, these internal conversations are useful. Leaders can develop an agenda for the first PLC+ team meeting to ensure that these matters are discussed.

COMMUNITY

In addition to highlighting the instructional leader and the PLC+ team, identify other key personnel a new teacher needs to know. For instance, are there special education specialists, language specialists, counselors, or other support people the new teacher will interact with right away? New teachers are not going to have contact with all the members of the professional learning community, so it is helpful for leaders to both check in and be available as new teachers need support or access to people and other resources.

In addition, communication norms within and across PLC+ teams are vital for success. In order to deepen the social cohesion of the group, members need to utilize communication tools that signal active listening and supportive exchanges of ideas. Here are seven norms of collaborative work from cognitive coaching practices (Costa & Garmston, 2015), which are useful for developing communication skills in teams that address the relational elements essential to deep collaboration.

> In order to deepen the social cohesion of the group, members need to utilize communication tools that signal active listening and the supportive exchanges of ideas.

1. **Pausing to ensure that others are able to fully form their thoughts and put them into words.** (Think of this as wait time we use with students.) Pausing gives speakers time to consider their own ideas, and it signals to them and others that their contributions are valued.

2. **Paraphrasing to clarify what others are saying.** The speaker's statements are recast to ensure that what has been understood is accurate and complete.

3. **Posing questions.** Once an initial understanding has been reached, the group can pose questions. The first questions should further clarify the details, be factual in nature, and be closed in type, followed by open-ended questions to mediate the thinking of ourselves and others.

4. **Providing data to interrogate evidence of impact.** This requires data discussion that strives to find the story behind the data. This is especially important when the data are quantitative, as the numbers can eclipse the humans it represents, and the context in which it was gathered.

5. **Putting ideas on the table.** In order to interrogate ideas without masking them, use neutral language to separate the idea from the person.

6. **Paying attention to self and others.** This includes noting nonverbal language, gestures, and body language.

7. **Presuming positive intentions.** This refers to reframing when someone expresses frustration. After all, no one gets frustrated about things they don't care about.

PAUSE AND PONDER

What existing PLC+ teams are especially strong in their communication skills? Are there teams that need a bit more attention? How might you situate supports for weaker teams who also have new teachers?

ACADEMIC GOALS

PLC+ teams often have ways of working together and processes that may be unfamiliar to a new teacher. This is likely to be the case when it comes to identifying a common challenge, navigating the investigation cycle, proceeding to gather evidence, sharing it within the team, and sharing it across the schoolwide professional learning community. If you have a group of new teachers, including those who are new to the school, you might consider forming them as a PLC+ team early in the school year so they can identify a common challenge that is specific to their learning. In these cases, it can also be useful to place an experienced activator in a group of new teachers so the PLC+ process can be accurately modeled. While this advice differs from our general practice of developing activators from within the team, it is wise to consider the overall benefits of learning the process correctly from the beginning. As the fictional character Mary Poppins advised, "Well begun is half done."

PROFESSIONAL GROWTH

Exposure to PLC+ teams often highlights needs a new teacher wasn't initially aware of, such as learning about how to create more discussion-based learning or the best ways to implement a complex math strategy. This is also true of teachers who are not new to the profession but who are new to the school site.

Encourage new teachers to discuss their professional needs with you as the instructional leader. Strong relationships develop through trust and open communication. A culture of feedback occurs when instructional leaders regularly solicit and listen to individual teachers. Learn about the interests of teachers at your school by hosting individual meetings with each to discuss their personalized learning for the year. When you know what each teacher is interested in pursuing, you obtain a more nuanced understanding of the organization's newer members. In addition, this information can help you assist them by building informal networks among the staff, pairing those with similar learning goals.

Figure 12.2 offers a suggested discussion frame for teachers to complete in advance of meeting with you. When you support their personalized learning plans for growth, you make a true investment in the professional capital of the school (Hargreaves & Fullan, 2012).

> Encourage new teachers to discuss their professional needs with you as the instructional leader.

FIGURE 12.2

PERSONALIZED LEARNING FOR NEW TEACHERS

PROPOSAL FOR PERSONALIZED PROFESSIONAL LEARNING

What is your personal learning goal for this school year?	I want to learn about . . . I want to strengthen my practice by . . . I want to teach others about . . .
How will you know you have been successful in achieving your goal?	
How will you demonstrate evidence of your learning?	

WHAT SPECIFIC PROFESSIONAL LEARNING EXPERIENCES WILL YOU UTILIZE?

Online course:	Date range:
Webinars:	Date(s):
Content repository:	Name(s):
E-learning platforms (e.g., Twitter Education Chats, Facebook Live broadcasts, district social media interest groups):	Name(s):
Coaching-intensive platform:	Date range:
Who is your accountability partner?	
Is there a financial cost?	

Source: Fisher, Frey, Smith, and Hattie (2020, p. 56).

SELF-ASSESSMENT

How will you support novice teachers and those who are new to your school site? Use the grid below to customize a list of information, resources, and supports that can be utilized to support them. Keep in mind that you are not the only resource. What are the professional learning community and its teams able to offer? What supports should you or your leadership be equipped to do?

	BASIC NEEDS	EXPECTATIONS	COMMUNITY	ACADEMIC GOALS	PROFESSIONAL GROWTH
What do new teachers need to know?					
What is the best timing for this?					
Who is responsible for this? Who will ensure that the component is inclusive and well-received by the new teacher?					
How and when will messages be reinforced?					

Source: Adapted from TNTP (2013).

Visit the companion website at
resources.corwin.com/PLC+forleaders
for downloadable resources.

Idea 12: Teachers new to the profession or to the school require attention for the PLC to thrive.

NOTES

Idea 13

LEADERS CAN ASSIST PLC+ TEAMS IN DETERMINING THEIR IMPACT.

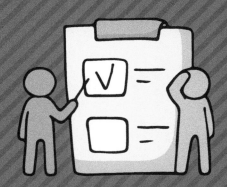

Essential Question: What structures are in place in your school so that PLC+ teams understand their impact?

An important task of school leaders is to help PLC+ teams determine the impact of their work on their students' learning and on their own learning. This process helps them build their collective teacher efficacy, and it communicates valuable findings across the schoolwide professional learning community.

PAUSE AND PONDER

Do PLC+ teams know how to determine the impact of their work? What are current strengths of the teams? What are areas of growth?

DETERMINING IMPACT

Throughout this guide, we have been very intentional about highlighting the importance of PLC+ teams as a means to foster collective teacher efficacy and the professional capital of the school. Hattie (2023) notes that efficacy is sustained not through feel-good sessions but through opportunities to engage in collaborative inquiry that requires the following:

- Expertise of sensitivity

- Noticing that a critical event requires attention

- Interpretation to make sense of the event

- Reasoning using evidence to move beyond opinions

- A repertoire of strategies

- Allowing for multiple voices to make interpretations

- Skills to navigate tensions

- Challenging and critiquing one's own and others' viewpoints

- Confidence that the collective can lead to a better interpretation and direction

- Judgment to choose the best course of action (p. 228)

One simple but significant way to guide teams is to be cognizant of what is the most important focus area for them instructionally—their common challenge. Ensure that they are intentionally monitoring their classroom actions for attaining the common challenge. Ask them about the evidence they are collecting to best determine their success. And always encourage them to interrogate assumptions they may have that block their view of what is really happening. Far too often teams get distracted from examining the evidence that is most relevant to their common challenge because they are not intentional in their interrogation processes.

PROCESSES THAT SUPPORT NOTICING

The school improvement plan at Northside Elementary School includes a focus on number sense based on previous years' data analysis. The second-grade PLC+ team is focusing on a common challenge to develop their students' skills and conceptual understanding to determine equivalent fractions from a given fraction. As their unit begins, the team focuses intently on using PLC+ Question 3—*How do we move learning forward?*—to identify classroom instructional actions and provide specific feedback to their students related to determining equivalent fractions.

The team administers an assessment that has specific items about equivalent fractions and other previously learned math concepts. Here is the breakdown of how their students perform:

Number of Items	Number and Percentage of Students Above 80% (12 or More Correct) on Entire Assessment
15	67 out of 108 students (62%) reached a score of 80%

This is an example of a situation where leaders and activators need to guide teams to make sure they don't miss an opportunity to build upon their collective efficacy. The dialogue below shows how it's especially important for leaders and activators to ensure that the team doesn't focus on a superficial finding and then move immediately to action without conducting a deeper analysis.

As the team focuses on determining the impact of their instruction, they have the following conversation:

Joan (core activator):	Okay, team. Steve has assembled all of our data from our Unit 3 mini-assessment. What are some inferences we can draw from the data as a whole?
Steve:	I am so frustrated! I felt we worked so hard last week getting kids ready for the assessment, and then just a little more than half are proficient or higher!
Juanita:	I know. I felt so confident going into the assessment last week, and I wonder now how I missed seeing where they were.
Joan (core activator):	I understand. Does anyone else have any thoughts?
Ken:	Wait a minute, team. I think we are missing something. What was our common challenge? To make sure that above all else, our kids can determine equivalent fractions from a given fraction, correct? And that was what we really focused on, right? If we look closely at the assessment questions, questions 3, 4, 6, 9, and 10 are specific to that. Can we take a moment and see how well they did *just* on those items?

After a few minutes, the team calculates the evidence again, this time with a focus on the equivalent fraction items.

Number of Items	Items Specifically Aligned to Determining Equivalent Fractions	Number/ Percentage of Students Above 80% (12 or More Correct) on Entire Assessment	Number/ Percentage Proficient or Above on Items Specific to Equivalent Fractions
15	3, 4, 6, 9, 10	67/108 (62%)	104/108 (96%)

It's especially important for leaders and activators to ensure that the team doesn't focus on a superficial finding and then move immediately to an action without conducting a deeper analysis.

Steve and Juanita (simultaneously):	Wow! I knew it.
Steve:	Look at that! Look at what we can do when we focus on something. Sure, we still have work to do, but knowing that what we did really worked makes me proud.
Joan (core activator):	We're not done, though. If we don't look at our initial assessment data, then we're making an assumption that nobody knew how to solve for equivalent fractions before we started this unit.
Ken (now serving as an additional activator):	Thanks for saying that. We need to do a deeper dive to find out which kids made progress, even if they didn't master it completely, and which kids didn't make progress they because already knew it and didn't make gains. I'll make a chart for us so we can start going deeper. [See Figure 13.1.]
Joan (core activator):	You're right. We can't understand who benefited and who did not. Module 18 [in the *PLC+ Playbook*] has more on how to do this. Let's use that to keep our discussion going.

FIGURE 13.1

CHART OF ACHIEVEMENT VERSUS PROGRESS

HIGHER ACHIEVEMENT, LIMITED PROGRESS	HIGHER ACHIEVEMENT, SIGNIFICANT PROGRESS
LOWER ACHIEVEMENT, LIMITED PROGRESS	LOWER ACHIEVEMENT, SIGNIFICANT PROGRESS

Source: Fisher et al. (2019b, p. 122).

Teams can get stuck in gathering superficial evidence of impact, and in doing so they may miss deepening their understanding of what is really happening. How do you advise teams who accept results too quickly? What data gathering, analysis, and reporting processes are embedded in PLC+ teams to prevent this?

CONFIDENCE THAT THE COLLECTIVE CAN LEAD TO A BETTER INTERPRETATION AND DIRECTION

The history department at North High School has formed a PLC+ team made up of several teachers within the department. All teach different courses, including U.S. history, world history, and government. The common challenge they have embraced, guided by the school's campus improvement plan, is to support their students to be able to analyze evidence from multiple sources to make strong claims and arguments. Accordingly, they have each embedded principles of claims and arguments into their content-specific instruction.

After visualizing the data to look more closely at progress and achievement, they are able to better see who benefited and who did not from the first unit. They share their findings with the schoolwide professional learning community through a gallery walk, inviting other teams to ask questions and make suggestions. Among the advice they get is to talk to students about their impressions.

They then decide that their next investigation cycle should focus on locating what was working for students who made progress regardless of whether they had fully mastered this complex set of skills. They determine that this will allow them to better target those students who made only limited progress. One of the data collection tools they use, as suggested by other members of the school community, is to form focus groups of students who made progress to find out what was working for them. In addition, they talk to individual students who didn't make progress to better understand barriers that might be interfering with their learning.

As they progress through the second cycle, they realize that it wasn't that their students knew more about the content related to World War II, or more about microeconomics versus macroeconomics, and so forth. Instead, they see that their students have substantially improved in their ability to *use* content knowledge and information to make stronger claims and arguments. When the team shares their impact with the schoolwide community after the second cycle, they are able to pair their evidence of impact with recommendations for what worked, further contributing to the spread of innovation.

Here are some of the solid recommendations the team makes to their colleagues across the school based on their determination of their impact.

1. Focus intentionally on every unit and provide feedback to students more on the quality of the evidence they are using in their argument, rather than just on content.

2. Intentionally use collaborative learning and discussion techniques on a regular basis (multiple times per week for at least fifteen-minute intervals), where students share their critical thinking in their arguments with each other.

3. Ensure that students use a solid protocol for challenging each other to bring up the best possible evidence and counterarguments.

How do you currently guide PLC+ teams to utilize common challenges as a means to gather specific evidence of their impact? How do the common challenges teams focus on align with your campus's or district improvement plan's initiatives or focus areas?

SELF-ASSESSMENT

Teams can miss gathering evidence of impact when they deviate from their agreed common challenge. A useful tool PLC+ teams can use to organize their thinking is the common challenge–determining impact tool below. This organizer provides a way for teams to stay on course not just by doing, but by analyzing and reflecting on what they did. We've completed one row as an example.

COMMON CHALLENGE-DETERMINING IMPACT TOOL

DISTRICT OR SCHOOL IMPROVEMENT PLAN FOCUS	PLC+ TEAM COMMON CHALLENGE	SPECIFIC INSTRUCTIONAL ACTIONS AND APPROACHES TAKEN	MOST RELEVANT STUDENT LEARNING EVIDENCE	EVIDENCE OF IMPACT TO SHARE
Campus Improvement Plan Data Analysis indicated a need to focus on reading comprehension, specifically close reading of informational texts.	Career and Technical Education PLC+ is made up of a variety of disciplines: Masonry, Family and Consumer Sciences Education, Nursing, Auto-Mechanics, and Apprenticeship to Plumbing. Focused on strategies and actions for students to navigate technical texts for coursework as well as for some advanced certification for possible job placement after high school.	• Intentionally modeling using "Stretch Texts" while providing advanced organizers (effect size = 0.41) • Supporting students in rereading deliberately while noticing confusing concepts • Cornell Note Taking • Focused peer-peer discussions (effect size = 0.82)	Monthly assessment evidence End of unit and course assessments (some that were externally administered)	Students grew considerably over the year, and the team noted that the percentage of students passing externally administered assessments related to their certifications increased from 74% to 91% in one year.

Visit the companion website at
resources.corwin.com/PLC+forleaders
for downloadable resources.

Idea 14

LEADERS SPREAD INNOVATIONS ACROSS THE SCHOOLWIDE PLC+.

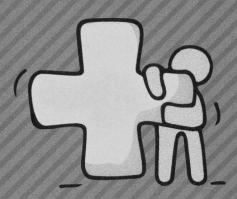

Essential Question: What are some ways to spread effective teaching and learning strategies across the schoolwide professional learning community?

While change can be viewed as exciting and renewing by some teachers, others may experience feelings of being overwhelmed or even fearful. These emotions are natural because we're creatures of habit. When educators hear the words "change initiative" because test scores have dipped, or when they hear that there's going to be a district improvement plan because there's a new superintendent—whatever the situation may be—it is invariably followed by uneasiness about what the future may hold.

Change is a process, not an event. Understanding change processes actually speeds innovation (Lassiter et al., 2022). Effective instructional leaders anticipate concerns about change and acknowledge that these perceptions are valid. At the same time, they lead change in ways that are humane and growth producing. Importantly, they communicate that the change isn't a buffet of items teachers might choose to select (or not). Rather, it is a necessary process supported by evidence of impact at the local level.

Just as importantly, leaders don't implement change alone. Hord and colleagues, in their 1984 study of schools and change, noted that in all cases school leaders worked with "change facilitators" to spread innovation effectively across the school. Although this study is several decades old, we cite it as an early example of how professional learning communities were already being conceived as a vehicle of change, with school leaders and change facilitators dedicated to moving adult learning forward.

In your experience, how is change perceived by your school staff? What are some of the more common anxieties or hesitations expressed? How do you approach these concerns?

HOW IS CHANGE SPREAD?

By communicating and creating conditions for PLC+ teams to forge their own paths in relation to professional learning, instructional leaders can reduce or eliminate much of the anxiety that typically accompanies change. We call these efforts *innovations* because evidence of impact should result in greater student learning *and* adult learning.

Greenhalgh et al. (2004) investigated the characteristics of organizations that anticipated change as a necessary condition for gaining positive results. They wondered how some organizations managed to avoid "bad ideas"—did they just get lucky? Their extensive review of the literature revealed three key ideas that explain why change takes root in some organizations but not in others: *let it happen* (diffusion), *help it happen* (dissemination), or *make it happen* (implementation).

Figure 14.1 summarizes the characteristics of each approach.

FIGURE 14.1

THREE WAYS INNOVATION MIGHT SPREAD THROUGH AN ORGANIZATION

Diffusion	Dissemination	Implementation
• Passive • Unplanned • Untargeted	• Targeted distribution of information and materials to a specific audience	• Use of strategies to adopt and integrate interventions and change practice patterns
"Let It Happen"	*"Help It Happen"*	*"Make It Happen"*

Source: Adapted from Greenhalgh et al. (2004).

Let's look at each of these ways a bit further.

DIFFUSION: LET IT HAPPEN

When an instructional leader doesn't have a communication plan for explaining, discussing, and spreading the innovations crafted by PLC+ teams in response to a common challenge, the innovations feel random and may be shrugged off by other teams. Consequently, it's unlikely that other teams will be exposed to, understand, and possibly be willing to try the innovation for themselves. This is diffusion: communication is passive, unplanned, and untargeted (Greenhalgh et al., 2004). In these situations, the instructional leader can only hope that a team's PLC+ team's learning will be diffused to other teams. At best, knowledge gained will be scattered about—but not shared. In short, diffusion is a highly ineffective strategy to foster collective teacher efficacy.

DISSEMINATION: HELP IT HAPPEN

Instructional leaders who employ a dissemination approach are more strategic (Greenhalgh et al., 2004). They set up horizontal and vertical structures to help spread information and knowledge. The leaders also set formal expectations for interactions around common challenges and innovations such that educators have opportunities to discuss the essence of the innovation as well as the details related to instruction and student learning. Interpersonal influence occurs during dissemination because educators can visualize how an innovation could look in their own classrooms.

Success in
a similar
context is
alluring and
encourages
other
teachers to
take notice.

With this approach, a sense of collective responsibility is fostered for all the students at the school, not just the ones on a teacher's current roster. Success in a similar context is alluring and encourages other teachers to take notice. Leaders arrange formal structures to share knowledge, such as World Cafe and gallery walks, which we will discuss in more detail later in this section. Dissemination is a useful strategy for promoting both teacher credibility and collective teacher efficacy.

IMPLEMENTATION: MAKING IT HAPPEN

Implementation occurs when the instructional leader creates the conditions that inspire PLC+ teams to take what they've learned vicariously during dissemination and apply it in their own classrooms. During dissemination, people often think to themselves, "*I could do that*" and express an interest to learn more because they recognize the value of the innovation on student and adult learning. They see their colleagues energized by their innovations, and they want similar experiences. The hallmark of implementation is when other teams take on a similar common challenge and apply the same evidence-based strategy with their own students, adjusting as necessary to ensure student success. This is how change can positively permeate a school community. The mechanisms for dissemination and implementation are critical components to spreading innovations that are worthy of students' learning, enhance teacher credibility, and foster collective teacher efficacy.

NOTES

_____

_____

_____

_____

_____

_____

_____

_____

_____

_____

_____

When you consider your school's structures for PLC+ teams to communicate their common challenges and innovations, where do you fall on the diffusion-dissemination-implementation continuum?

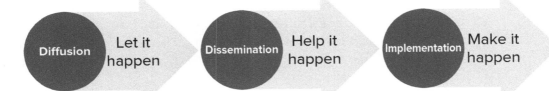

If you rated yourself toward the diffusion side of the continuum, thank you for being honest! We have to start somewhere. What are one or two actions you could take to begin to structure opportunities for dissemination a few times per school year?

If you're closer to the middle of the continuum, what barriers might be in the way of providing dissemination opportunities for PLC+ teams? What are one or two actions you could take to remove those barriers? For instance, would it be helpful to touch base with activators and gather their input about structuring formal dissemination opportunities in the future?

If you have formal structures for dissemination but you aren't seeing implementation, what might be some of the causes? What could you do, or who might you recruit to support you with these efforts?

FORMAL STRUCTURES TO SPREAD INNOVATIONS

School leaders recognize the value of clear, ongoing, and proactive communication within the school. The PLC+ framework offers many opportunities for teams to learn horizontally, vertically, and across the whole school as a professional learning community. This marks a shift from traditional professional development events and staff meetings, often considered stale or disconnected, and instead holds student and adult learning at the center of these efforts. Leaders collaborate with PLC+ teams to design and schedule three or four formal opportunities to disseminate knowledge each school year, depending on whether the school calendar is organized by quarters or trimesters. These occasions promote professional learning that enhances teacher credibility, collective responsibility, and collective teacher efficacy.

The learning of PLC + teams can spread throughout the school community and to other campuses as well. Imagine the response from parents, siblings, and families who are invited to the school to gain a deeper understanding of what their children are learning in the classroom each day. Relationships between school staff and families are likely to deepen as opportunities for true partnerships in the learning process are established. This practice encourages stronger levels of family engagement because the school extends bridges to students' educational experiences regularly, not just when sharing a report card, which is often done as a one-way conversation from teacher to caregiver.

> **Relationships between school staff and families are likely to deepen as opportunities for true partnerships in the learning process are established.**

There's no one right way to structure formal dissemination of knowledge experiences, but there are two key aspects:

1. Ensure that there are protocols in place that foster reflection and facilitate healthy dialogue.

2. Put these occasions on the calendar before the school year begins so that families can plan their attendance and staff can become familiar with the routine of regular formal dissemination. When we regularly engage in a routine, it becomes a habit.

As leaders, we strive for conversations about learning to be the part and parcel way of doing business that defines the school culture. As noted earlier, two dissemination practices we have implemented with great success are gallery walks and World Cafes.

GALLERY WALKS

A gallery walk is a discussion technique for small groups to engage with the ideas of others. In the case of PLC+ teams, this technique is used so that each team can profile their work on a poster, listing their common challenge, the techniques they used, and their findings. Teacher teams rotate around the room, viewing and discussing each poster. They may leave sticky notes posing further questions, making recommendations, or linking to other work.

Gallery walks can be designed for an in-person event, but team posters can be displayed for a period of time. Some schools have common areas or hallways where team members' posters are displayed for a given number of weeks. Gallery walks can also be done virtually, with each PLC+ team developing a collaborative slide explaining their work. These slides are placed in a virtual space, such as Google Drive, for each team to view the work of others.

Posters that are designed for gallery walks may include information the PLC+ team gathered during their investigation of the common challenge. They may note the evidence-based strategies and resources used to gain expertise for its implementation. Many teams include actual student work samples, images, and QR (quick-response) codes leading to videos of their practice.

It is crucial for the professional learning community as a whole to discuss what they have noticed, learned, and wonder about after the gallery walk is concluded. While the gallery walk process is good for dissemination, implementation is unlikely to take hold unless there is further discussion about implications and future work regarding promising practices.

WORLD CAFE

The World Cafe method is a flexible and effective format for promoting dialogue among large groups of people. This is an iterative process, meaning that the decisions reached in one World Cafe session inform the next session to be held weeks later. This methodology was developed by Brown (2002) in her dissertation on communication in human and organizational systems. It is an innovative form of conversational inquiry and knowledge creation that moves teams to action using design principles of idea generation (see Figure 14.2):

- Reflection and exploration to learn about the perspectives and experiences of others

- Collective insights to note similarities and differences

- Harvesting discoveries to summarize emerging thoughts and ideas

- Action planning about the next steps

- Implementation to apply new ideas in other settings

- Feedback and assessment to determine successes and revisions

FIGURE 14.2

THE WORLD CAFE MODEL

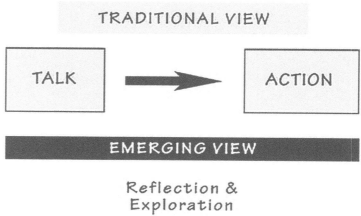

TRADITIONAL VIEW

TALK → ACTION

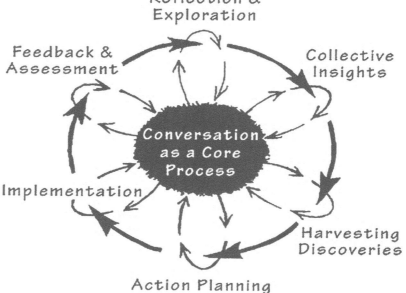

EMERGING VIEW

Reflection & Exploration

Feedback & Assessment

Collective Insights

Conversation as a Core Process

Implementation

Harvesting Discoveries

Action Planning

Source: The World Cafe, https://theworldcafe.com

We use World Cafe principles as a means to disseminate the learning of PLC+ teams across the schoolwide professional learning community and spark implementation. In the World Cafe approach, a host from each PLC+ team disseminates knowledge to a small group of educators across multiple rounds of 20 minutes or so. According to the team at the World Cafe (n.d.), there are five components to the method:

- **Setting.** Create a special environment similar to what you might see in your favorite café. While it's not necessary to be fancy, educators often appreciate a little sparkle. We suggest using small round tables with markers, large chart paper, and a vase of flowers placed on each table. Usually there are four or five chairs at each table, facilitating an intimate environment for dialogue. Encourage people to doodle, write, and draw their insights, questions, and wonderings on the chart paper. This serves as a place of knowledge creation for each subsequent round of participants as they read and integrate prior comments into their conversation.

- **Welcome and introduction.** The table host (one PLC+ team member per table) opens with a warm welcome and sets the context of the process. Table hosts switch for each round so that everyone gets to participate in multiple rounds. Table leaders can use the Common Challenge–Determining Impact Tool (Figure 13.2) to guide their conversation.

- **Small group rounds.** Dissemination of knowledge begins with the first of three or more twenty-minute rounds of conversation around each table. At the end of the twenty minutes, each person moves to a different table of their own choice. In other words, the composition of a group during the first round of World Cafe is not necessarily the same composition in the next round. Team hosts also switch out from one round to the next so that they can join the next series of conversations at other tables.

- **Questions.** Each round is focused on the question that drove the team's investigation of the common challenge. The host provides this context and guides the direction of the conversation such that it focuses on student and adult learning.

- **Harvest.** In between rounds, as well as at the end of the rounds, participants are invited to share insights with one another that emerged during the World Cafe. Typically, teachers will have participated in three or four rounds, exposing them to several common challenges in the innovations teams crafted to address student needs. After a few minutes of individual reflection, larger conversations are opened for the whole staff, inviting educators to hear others' impressions and considerations. The instructional leader or another facilitator will capture the conversations either in writing or by video so there is a record of professional learning and opportunities for people to watch the World Cafe.

We suggest trying a protocol such as a gallery walk, World Cafe, or other formal structure of your choice for the first year or two in your PLC+ journey. Given that these dissemination opportunities occur three or four times per year, educators will have time to grow accustomed to a routine. Over time, your school may innovate on dissemination practices as the staff becomes more accustomed to the expectation that evidence of impact and innovation is regularly shared across the school. This approach fosters continuous learning at all levels because people do not have to remember a new routine; the common challenges change, but the structures for dissemination and implementation do not. Figure 14.3 contains two examples of how PLC+ teams used a World Cafe or a gallery walk to profile their findings across the professional learning community.

FIGURE 14.3

EXAMPLES OF FORMAL STRUCTURES TO DISSEMINATE KNOWLEDGE AND FOSTER FUTURE INNOVATIONS

DISSEMINATION ACTIVITY	PLC+ TEAM COMMON CHALLENGE	SPECIFIC INSTRUCTIONAL ACTIONS AND APPROACHES TAKEN	MOST RELEVANT STUDENT LEARNING EVIDENCE	EVIDENCE OF IMPACT TO SHARE
World Cafe	Eighth-grade ELA: Our students are having difficulty analyzing and discussing language choices in grade-level narrative texts.	Juicy Sentence protocol Close reading Collaborative conversations	Videos of collaborative conversations while students worked in pairs to unpack a complex sentence	Student work samples of the meanings of analyzed texts; demonstration of understanding by justifying, persuading, or evaluating an author's word choices; measures of Lexile growth pre- and post-investigation cycle
Gallery Walk	Interdisciplinary high school team: Students are struggling to design and fulfill meaningful service learning projects.	Taught a structured framework to students for organizing, managing, and evaluating service learning projects Created weekly check-in progress report times for troubleshooting projects Used community organizers as outside evaluators	Photographs and video footage of five student service learning projects posted to the Aurasma-augmented reality platform	Comparative data of previous evaluations of student learning projects last year compared to this year Students' self-evaluations of their projects Outside community evaluators' results

FROM DISSEMINATION TO IMPLEMENTATION

If professional learning sessions like gallery walks and World Cafe are viewed simply as a nice time together, then implementation is not going to take hold. It is essential to follow up with the schoolwide professional learning community to distill the knowledge generated and apply it more widely to practice. Naturally, if the PLC+ teams at your site are investigating different common challenges, then the innovations developed may have a more limited range. For instance, a science department's common challenge about how their students are able to analyze lab data may not be meaningful for the English department. In other cases, a schoolwide common challenge on the development of academic language for multilingual learners would have wider implications. Both are of value; the scope of application varies.

Once the dissemination phase of the professional learning community is done, it is time to discuss implications and future applications of knowledge. After summarizing the findings of each PLC+, lead the faculty through a decision-making exercise that emphasizes implementation and de-implementation. The latter is sometimes necessary because unlearning may be needed. For instance, ending the harmful practice of round-robin reading is an example of de-implementation. Use Figure 14.4 to lead this discussion with the faculty. We've completed one row for you as an example.

> It is essential to follow up with the schoolwide professional learning community to distill the knowledge generated and apply it more widely to practice.

NOTES

_____

_____

_____

_____

_____

_____

_____

_____

_____

_____

_____

_____

_____

_____

_____

FIGURE 14.4

HOW WILL WE USE WHAT WE HAVE LEARNED?

NEW LEARNING 1	EVIDENCE OF IMPACT	ACTIONS
Daily use of the 3-read protocol across content areas improved informational text comprehension.	Seventh-grade team implemented this for 18 weeks and saw an average of 52 Lexile point gain among students, compared to an expected gain of 31.5 points.	**KEEP** regular use of informational texts in classes.
		STOP assigning reading without further guidance and expecting that somehow students will "get it."
		START using a daily 3-read protocol in all classes for short pieces of text.

NEW LEARNING 2	EVIDENCE OF IMPACT	ACTIONS
		KEEP
		STOP
		START

SELF-ASSESSMENT

Let's circle back to your actions. It is likely that some of the actions you have been taking as they apply to leading PLC+ schoolwide are really working for you, while other actions are not. Reflect on your leadership actions as they relate to fueling innovation at the site level. What do you want to keep doing? Stop doing? Start doing? How will you use what you are learning?

NEW LEARNING 1	EVIDENCE OF IMPACT	ACTIONS
		KEEP
		STOP
		START

NEW LEARNING 2	EVIDENCE OF IMPACT	ACTIONS
		KEEP
		STOP
		START

Visit the companion website at
resources.corwin.com/PLC+forleaders
for downloadable resources.

NOTES

Idea 15

LEADERS NEED TO COMMUNICATE IMPACT TO STAKEHOLDERS BEYOND THE PROFESSIONAL LEARNING COMMUNITY.

Essential Question: How do you ensure that external stakeholders— including families, other schools, district leaders, and the superintendent—know about innovations at your school?

You've probably heard the adage, "Don't hide your light under a bushel." It's often interpreted as a reminder that personal accomplishments should be shared. But in this case, our advice has to do with spreading innovation beyond a single site. After all, school improvement is really about strengthening the community and the district.

Handford and Leithwood (2019) performed an extensive review of the literature to understand the influence of school districts on students' mathematics and reading achievement. They noted that these nine conditions were evident in high-performing districts (p. 3):

1. Broadly shared mission, vision, and goals founded on ambitious images of an educated person

2. Coherent instructional guidance

3. Deliberate and consistent use of multiple sources of evidence to inform decisions

4. Learning-oriented organizational improvement processes

5. Professional development for all members

6. Alignment of budgets, personnel policies/procedures, and uses of time with district mission, vision, and goals

7. A comprehensive approach to professional leadership development

8. Policy-oriented district of trustees or school board

9. Productive working relationships with staff and stakeholders

Many of these conditions inform and are informed by a PLC+ team who seeks to identify the common challenge, use evidence to inform practice, and view themselves as an organization that learns. The researchers further noted that these conditions are hampered without strong internal structures that view school sites as sources of information and innovation for system improvement. In particular, they advised that districts develop internal communication systems consisting of the following actions (p. 4):

1. Develop communication systems and processes throughout the district to keep all members informed

2. Develop open, accessible, and collaborative relationships with principals

3. Encourage reciprocal forms of communication with and among schools

4. Promote high levels of interaction among all school leaders, driven by a shared sense of responsibility for system improvement

Communication is at the heart of the PLC+ framework.

Many districts have innovative practices that are inhibited because they are unintentionally well-kept secrets. Consequently, they remain as silos of excellence. Leaders and teachers outside those buildings aren't aware of the learning at a single school site, and thus system-level changes never happen. Their light stays under that bushel basket. Having said that, school site leaders need communication competence to communicate impact outside the walls of their individual schools.

PAUSE AND PONDER

Communication is at the heart of the PLC+ framework. If you are a district leader, to what extent are successes shared across school sites? If you are a site-based leader, do you communicate successes to stakeholders outside the school organization? Use Handford and Leithwood's (2019) list of four internal communication structures to consider current strengths and growth opportunities.

DEVELOP EFFECTIVE COMMUNICATION STRATEGIES

District leaders are often the ones who lead the charge of professional learning and development initiatives. They need to be kept abreast of successes happening in schools so that they may be better equipped at guiding school leaders at other sites who are struggling to overcome some of the same challenges. If you are a site leader, you are a key contributor to this communication channel. In addition, you have many external stakeholders who have different needs—families, district leaders, and the school board, to name a few. While some are internal stakeholders (students and staff), these external stakeholders require different kinds of communication. It's not that they have less interest, but they are not as knowledgeable about day-to-day operations. It is essential to be able to communicate to external stakeholders about how PLC+ efforts are aligned to district and school goals and initiatives.

CASEL, a major organization dedicated to social and emotional learning, understands the need to communicate initiatives to a variety of external stakeholders. They advise taking a four-step approach to communication, which was developed for them by the Collaborative Communications Group (2023), an organization that specializes in communication strategies for the educational field. Whether you are a district or site leader, these practices can be useful in framing ideas and communicating them effectively.

1. Who do you want to reach?

2. What do you want to achieve?

3. What do you want to say?

4. How will you send your message?

PAUSE AND PONDER

How would you rate your level of experience with preparing and delivering formal communications outside your school? What do you consider to be your strengths in these instances?

STEP 1: WHO DO YOU WANT TO REACH?

Identify who the external stakeholders are beyond the faculty and students in your school.

Communications should be tailored to the audience. Therefore, the first step is to identify who the external stakeholders are beyond the faculty and students in your school. For instance, district central office leaders are an important audience; so are the families of your students. But while each group is important, how the information is consumed and understood is going to be different. Possible external stakeholders to consider keeping apprised of the efforts of your professional learning community include the following:

- Families of students at your school

- Community organizations

- Central office administrators, including curriculum specialists

- Senior district leadership, including members of the superintendent's cabinet

- School board members

Communication with the school board is especially important in this context. Many school boards have a rolling agenda item that spotlights specific schools. If this is the case for you, consider how you might frame the work of your schoolwide professional learning community.

STEP 2: WHAT DO YOU WANT TO ACHIEVE?

Stakeholder mapping is useful for further identifying what you want to achieve in your communication. This technique is used by policy developers and project managers to identify key players who are essential to the success of the initiative or program (Aligica, 2006). Stakeholder mapping requires consideration of two conditions: their relative influence and their relative interest in the work of the professional learning community. Collaborative Communications Group advises not only listing who your stakeholders are but also engaging in these considerations (see Figure 15.1).

NOTES

Use Figure 15.1 to map external stakeholders you want to communicate with about issues relating to professional learning communities. Add the names of groups or individuals to the quadrants that best describe their relative influence and interest.

FIGURE 15.1

STAKEHOLDER MAPPING FOR COMMUNICATING INNOVATIONS

High Power, Low Interest	High Influence, High Interest
Keep Satisfied	*Manage Closely*
Low Power, Low Interest	High Interest, Low Power
Monitor	*Keep Informed*

Influence

Interest

STEP 3: WHAT DO YOU WANT TO SAY?

Once you have identified your external stakeholders and their degree of influence and interest, it's time to think about how you will craft your message. Think first in terms of timeliness and time invested. Depending on who you are speaking with or writing to, you are likely to have their attention for a finite amount of time. Addressing the school board, as one example, is probably going to come with a time limit. If you are communicating with families on the school website, they will probably have only a few minutes to read what you have written in your Principal's Message. Social media constraints are often even tighter—perhaps down to the number of characters you can use.

The content of the message is crucial, and distilling information can be time-consuming for you. However, the Common Challenge–Determining Impact Tool, introduced in Figure 13.2, can save you the time and effort needed to distill your message. When teams complete this tool to clarify their impact, they are also providing you with the information you need. We consider using this tool to be much more useful than relying on the laborious meeting minutes that teams are sometimes required to submit. The Common Challenge–Determining Impact Tool gives you a one- or two-page summary of the work of each team—and, most importantly, their impact.

As you analyze the summary, which efforts do you want to spotlight? This should be specific to the stakeholders you have identified. After all, the identical message isn't going to land with every group.

Collaborative Communications Group (2023) advises developing a message map to help you pare down your message to meet the needs of external stakeholders and your desired goals. This message map is composed of three elements: a core statement, key messages, and three supporting points.

The *core statement* is a one- or two-sentence summary that defines your message. Your core statement should engage your stakeholders immediately. If you are asking for something, say so. Fans of the television show *Shark Tank*, which focuses on budding entrepreneurs and potential investors, will recognize this approach. Here's an example of an effective attention-getter for district leaders:

> "Our school's PLC+ community is ensuring that innovation doesn't remain private practice. We invite district and school leaders to join us in a learning walk on February 15 as we demonstrate how we're using evidence-based strategies to promote reading comprehension at our middle school."

The *key messages* frame the topic by addressing the question, "What does that mean?" It's your opportunity to establish importance. An example would be

> "Middle school students face increasing demand for reading and understanding complex informational texts. We recognized that our students weren't making the kind of progress they needed to achieve. We launched a schoolwide investigation to identify what would make a difference to accelerate learning."

Provide three supporting points to reinforce your key message. These might be statistics regarding impact, or stories from teams and classrooms. That could look like this:

> "As an example, the seventh grade formed an interdisciplinary PLC+ team to investigate this issue. They agreed to use informational texts related to the content they were teaching and devoted 10 minutes each day to parsing out meaning using a 3-read protocol informed by the research on close readings of complex texts. In the span of eighteen weeks, they saw Lexile measures rise by an average of 52 points for their students. Impressive, considering that the average growth national for the entire seventh-grade year is 69 points. At this rate, they are projected to gain 104 Lexile points this year. This same strategy is now being used in sixth and eighth grades, where we hope to see similar acceleration."

Use the table in Figure 15.2 as a workspace to map your message.

NOTES

_____

_____

_____

_____

_____

_____

_____

_____

_____

_____

_____

_____

_____

_____

_____

_____

_____

_____

FIGURE 15.2

MAP YOUR MESSAGE WORKSPACE

What's the core statement for this stakeholder group? Make sure it engages them based on their interests and influence. If there is something you are asking for, say so.

What is the key message you want to convey?

What are three supporting points that back your claim?

Supporting Point 1	Supporting Point 2	Supporting Point 3

STEP 4: HOW WILL YOU SEND YOUR MESSAGE?

The steady rise of digital technologies has given us a plethora of communication outlets to augment face-to-face interactions. In addition to school board meetings and scheduled meetings with other school and district leaders, digital outlets can further your reach, especially to families and community organizations. Of course, you will want to be sure to tailor your message based on the outlet.

INFORM FAMILY AND COMMUNITY STAKEHOLDERS

Consider devoting a place on your school website to spotlight the work of PLC+ teams and the schoolwide professional learning community. Families are often mystified about what occurs on early release days and student-free days dedicated to professional learning. Craft messages that let them know about how the staff is learning together and, most importantly, why this benefits their child (placing the focus on the families' interest).

Digital message boards. Many schools have large digital announcement boards located in a public area of the school. Keep in mind that it's not just students and staff who read these messages. Families, vendors, delivery personnel, and district staff move in and out of your campus every day. Some schools may also have an outdoor electronic sign that scrolls through events. Add impact data—such as "Seventh graders gained 52 Lexile points in reading last semester, exceeding the average pace of readers around the country"—to let the community know about the successes happening at the school.

Social media outlets. Is your school on Facebook, Twitter, or Instagram? Update information with the efforts about PLC+ teams at your school to reach families, alumni, and other interested external stakeholders. Collaborative Communications Group (2023) advises that social media posts are carefully crafted (p. 17). Here's what they recommend.

- Official posts should be made by an identified individual who has been trained in the district's guidelines for social media usage.

- Think in multiple contexts. A comment that makes sense in one context could appear insensitive or ignorant in another.

- Write thoughtfully and carefully.

- Do not provide personal editorials on controversial topics. You are writing as a representative of the district.

- Make sure you have permission when using quotes, photos, or videos.

INFORM SCHOOL AND DISTRICT LEADERS

Having a system in place that allows for schools within and across districts to share ideas and examples of impact is critical to harness the power of effective PLC+ collaboration. This also ensures that the school and the district as a whole is the professional learning community. A PLC+ approach should not be narrowly defined as meetings.

Principal meetings. These are ideal times for sharing innovations across schools. Time should be devoted in each meeting to opportunities for school leaders to talk about the impact of PLC+ teams at their schools, as well as management issues related to the schoolwide professional learning community. If there are internal digital communication channels for leaders, these can also be used to provide further details about the work being accomplished.

System-level learning walks. Some districts already have processes established to conduct system-level learning walks to build district capacity. Schools take turns serving as the host and lead a learning walk focused on a single topic, and district and school leaders from other sites make short observations (10 minutes or so). The processes are quite similar to the teacher learning walks described in Idea 7. Consider conducting these walks when PLC+ teams are meeting. This can contribute to the capacity of site leaders as they navigate logistical issues and professional learning.

Senior district leadership. As schoolwide professional learning communities become more accustomed to disseminating and implementing innovation (Idea 14), consider inviting senior members of the district to observe and participate. For example, a World Cafe–style gathering can easily accommodate external stakeholders to learn alongside the PLC+ team. This provides yet another opportunity to see a PLC+ framework in action.

PAUSE AND PONDER

How does your school or district communicate impact beyond the walls of the school buildings and district offices? What are some actions you can take to build or augment your current system of communication with all stakeholders in your school community?

SELF-ASSESSMENT

Communicating impact to external stakeholders requires understanding what your key message is regarding your professional learning community. Use the instrument below to assess your preparations and identify people and actions to move learning forward across the district. Rate your readiness to message stakeholders using the following scale, with 1 being very much in need to 5 being strongly evident.

FACTOR	PEOPLE TO ENLIST	ACTIONS NEEDED
1. Mapped stakeholders. 〔1···2···3···4···5〕		
2. Identified key message. 〔1···2···3···4···5〕		
3. Developed a core statement. 〔1···2···3···4···5〕		
4. Gathered evidence for supporting point 1. 〔1···2···3···4···5〕		
5. Gathered evidence for supporting point 2. 〔1···2···3···4···5〕		
6. Gathered evidence for supporting point 3. 〔1···2···3···4···5〕		
7. Identified how the message will be shared. 〔1···2···3···4···5〕		

online resources

Visit the companion website at
resources.corwin.com/PLC+forleaders
for downloadable resources.

NOTES

CODA

There is a saying in professional learning that "the answer is in the room." The challenges that schools face are invariably ones that strain the professional capital of the caring adults working within the institution. But time and again, the human, social, and decisional capital of educators has been demonstrated to play a crucial role in school improvement:

- Developing community schools (Sanders et al., 2021)

- Professional learning in elementary schools (Snow et al., 2015)

- Large-scale elementary reading and mathematics initiatives (Bryk et al., 2010)

- Mathematics initiatives with high school teachers (Callingham et al., 2015)

- Improving teacher satisfaction (Melesse & Belay, 2022)

- Policy work on accountability (Fullan et al., 2015)

A major outcome of the PLC+ approach is to promote the professional capital of staff across school buildings and entire districts such that innovation can be spread to accelerate the learning of adults. We have developed this model using the extensive research on professional learning, adult learning, change theory, systems theory, and school improvement. Having said that, we don't suggest that we possess the answers that challenge schools. But we will offer that the answer is in the room. The wisdom of the collective, coupled with investigation cycles designed to spark creativity, can generate solutions that are locally based, culturally responsive, and grounded in evidence. And it allows us to stop using "buy-in" as a barrier to innovation. You don't need buy-in when you've got something much stronger: *commitment*.

REFERENCES

Aligica, P. D. (2006). Institutional and stakeholder mapping: Frameworks for policy analysis and institutional change. *Public Organization Review*, *6*, 79–90.

Ash, G. E., Kuhn, M. R., & Walpole, S. (2009). Analyzing "inconsistencies" in practice: Teachers' continued use of round robin reading. *Reading & Writing Quarterly*, *25*(1), 87–103.

Baker-Doyle, K. J. (2012). First-year teachers' support networks: Intentional professional networks and diverse professional allies. *New Educator*, *8*(1), 65–85.

Bandura, A. (1977). Self-efficacy: Toward a unifying theory of behavioral change. *Psychological Review, 84*(2), 191–215.

Bandura, A. (1993). Perceived self-efficacy in cognitive development and functioning. *Educational Psychologist*, *28*, 117–148.

Brown, J. (2002). *The world café: Living knowledge through conversations that matter* [Doctoral dissertation, Fielding Graduate Institute]. UMI ProQuest. https://www .proquest.com/pqdthss/docview/276286326/376ADBFBC6B34C8BPQ/1?accoun tid=13758

Bryk, A. S., Sebring, P. B., Allensworth, E., Luppescu, S., & Easton, J. Q. (2010). *Organizing schools for improvement: Lessons from Chicago.* University of Chicago Press.

Callingham, R., Beswick, K., & Ferme, E. (2015). An initial exploration of teachers' numeracy in the context of professional capital. *ZDM - Mathematics Education*, *47*(4), 549–560.

Censuswide. (2019). *2019 workplace learning report.* https://learning.linkedin.com/ content/dam/me/business/en-us/amp/learning-solutions/images/workplace-learning-report-2019/pdf/workplace-learning-report-2019.pdf

City, E., Elmore, R. F., Fiarman, S. E., & Teitel, L. (2009). *Instructional rounds in education: A network approach to improving teaching and learning.* Harvard Education Press.

Cockerell, L. (2008). *Creating magic: 10 common sense leadership strategies from a life at Disney.* Currency.

Collaborative Communications Group. (2023). *Building your strategy: Steps for developing effective social and emotional learning communication strategies.* https://drc .casel.org/blog/resource/developing-effective-social-and-emotional-learning-communication-strategies-for-your-district/

Costa, A. L., & Garmston, R. J. (2015). *Cognitive coaching: Developing self-directed leaders and learners* (3rd ed.). Rowman & Littlefield.

DuFour, R., & Eaker, R. E. (1998). *Professional learning communities at work: Best practices for enhancing student achievement.* ASCD.

Evans, M., Teasdale, R. M., Gannon-Slater, N., La Londe, P. G., Crenshaw, H. L., Greene, J. C., & Schwandt, T. A. (2019). How did that happen? Teachers' explanations for low test scores. *Teachers College Record, 121*(2), 1–40.

Fisher, A. T., Alder, J. G., & Avasalu, M. (1998). Lecturing performance appraisal criteria: Staff and student difference. *Australian Journal of Education, 42*(2), 153–168.

Fisher, D., Everlove, S., & Frey, N. (2009). Not just another literacy meeting. *Principal Leadership, 9*(9), 40–43.

Fisher, D., Frey, N., Almarode, J., Flories, K., & Nagel, D. (2019a). *PLC+: Better decisions and greater impact by design*. Corwin.

Fisher, D., Frey, N., Almarode, J., Flories, K., & Nagel, D. (2019b). *The PLC+ playbook: A hands-on guide to collectively improving student learning*. Corwin.

Fisher, D., Frey, N., & Smith, D. (2020). *The teacher credibility and collective efficacy playbook*. Corwin.

Fisher, D., Frey, N., Smith, D., & Hattie, J. (2020). *The distance learning playbook for school leaders: Leading for engagement and impact in any setting*. Corwin.

Fisher, D., Frey, N., Smith, D., & Hattie, J. (2021a). *Leading the rebound: 20+ must-dos to restart teaching and learning*. Corwin.

Fisher, D., Frey, N., Smith, D., & Hattie, J. (2021b). *Rebound, grades K–12: A playbook for rebuilding agency, accelerating learning recovery, and rethinking schools*. Corwin.

Fullan, M. (2001). *Leading in a culture of change*. Jossey-Bass.

Fullan, M., Rincón-Gallardo, S., & Hargreaves, A. (2015). Professional capital as accountability. *Education Policy Analysis Archives, 23*(14–17), 1–18.

García-Martínez, I., Montenegro-Rueda, M., Molina-Fernández, E., & Fernández-Batanero, J. M. (2021). Mapping teacher collaboration for school success. *School Effectiveness & School Improvement, 32*(4), 631–649.

Greenhalgh, T., Robert, G., Macfarlane, F., Bate, P., & Kyriakidou, O. (2004). Diffusion of innovations in service organizations: Systematic review and recommendations. *The Milbank Quarterly, 82*(4), 581–629.

Greenstein, L. (2019). *Overcoming assessment bias: Making assessment fair for all learners*. https://www.assessmentnetwork.net/2019/02/overcoming-assessment-bias-making-assessment-fair-for-all-learners

Guthridge, L. (2018, August 10). How to drive success with three little words. *Forbes Magazine*. https://www.forbes.com/sites/forbescoachescouncil/2018/08/10/how-to-drive-success-with-three-little-words/?sh=2ea77af74594

Handford, V., & Leithwood, K. (2019). School districts' contributions to students' math and language achievement. *International Journal of Education Policy & Leadership, 14*(10), 1–21.

Hargreaves, A., & Fullan, M. (2012). *Professional capital: Transforming teaching in every school*. Teachers College Press.

Hattie, J. (2023). *Visible learning: The sequel. A synthesis of over 2100 meta-analyses relating to achievement*. Routledge.

Hord, S. M. (1980). *Working together: Cooperation or collaboration?* The Research and Development Center for Teacher Education, University of Texas at Austin.

Hord, S. M. (1997). *Professional learning communities: Communities of continuous inquiry and improvement*. White paper issued by Southwest Educational Development Laboratory, Austin, TX. https://files.eric.ed.gov/fulltext/ED410659.pdf

Hord, S. M. (2004). Professional learning communities: An overview. In S. M. Hord (Ed.), *Learning together, leading together: Changing schools through professional learning communities* (pp. 5–14). Teachers College Press.

Hord, S. M., Stiegelbauer, S. M., & Hall, G. E. (1984). How principals work with other change facilitators. *Education and Urban Society, 17*(1), 89–109.

Hoy, W. K., & Tschannen-Moran, M. (2003). The conceptualization and measurement of faculty trust in schools: The omnibus T-Scale. In W. K. Hoy & C. G. Miskel (Eds.), *Studies in leading and organizing schools* (pp. 181–208). Information Age.

Knowles, M. S. (1990). *The adult learner: A neglected species* (4th ed). Gulf Publishing.

Knowles, M. S., Holton, E. F., III., & Swanson, R. A. (2012). *The adult learner* (7th ed.). Routledge.

Kruse, S., Seashore Louis, K., & Bryk, A. (1994). Building professional community in schools. *Issues in Restructuring Schools, 6*, 3–6.

Lassiter, C., Fisher, D., Frey, N., & Smith, D. (2022). *How leadership works: A playbook for instructional leaders.* Corwin.

Leana, C. (2011). The missing link in school reform. *Stanford Social Innovation Review, 9*(4), 30–35.

Maslow, A. H. (1943). A theory of human motivation. *Psychological Review, 50*(4), 370–396. https://doi.org/10.1037/h0054346

Maslow, A. H. (1969). Theory Z. *Journal of Transpersonal Psychology, 1*(2), 31–47.

Masood, S. (2021, January 18). *Shirley Hord on PLC.* https://youtu.be/ZgKrNkeiF-w

McGregor, D. (1960). *The human side of enterprise.* McGraw-Hill Book Company.

Melesse, T., & Belay, S. (2022). Uplifting teachers' professional capital through promoting engagement in professional learning: Mediating effect of teacher job satisfaction. *Cogent Education, 9*(1), 1–19.

Morse, J. J., & Lorsch, J. W. (1970). Beyond theory Y. *Harvard Business Review.* https://hbr.org/1970/05/beyond-theory-y

Myers, C. B. (1996, April). *Beyond the PDS: Schools as professional learning communities: A proposal based on an analysis of PDS efforts in the 1990s.* Paper presented at the annual meeting of the American Educational Research Association, New York City. https://files.eric.ed.gov/fulltext/ED400227.pdf

Myers, C. B., & Myers, L. K. (1995). *The professional educator: A new introduction to teaching and schools.* Wadsworth.

Nagel, D., Almarode, J., Fisher, D., Frey, N., & Flories, K. (2020). *The PLC+ activator's guide.* Corwin.

Nottingham, J. A. (2017) *The learning challenge: How to guide your students through the learning pit to achieve deeper understanding.* Sage.

Nuthall, G. (2007). *The hidden lives of learners.* NZCER Press.

Page, M. (n.d.). *Building an effective team.* https://www.michaelpage.ae/advice/management-advice/development-and-retention/building-effective-team

Plato. (1992). *Republic.* (C. D. E. Reeve, Trans.). Hatchette.

Richter, E., Lucksnat, C., Redding, C., & Richter, D. (2022). Retention intention and job satisfaction of alternatively certified teachers in their first year of teaching. *Teaching & Teacher Education*, *114*, 103704. https://doi.org/10.1016/j.tate.2022.103704

Robinson, V. (2011). *Student-centered leadership*. Jossey-Bass.

Robinson, V. M., Lloyd, C. A., & Rowe, K. J. (2008). The impact of leadership on student outcomes: An analysis of the differential effects of leadership types. *Educational Administration Quarterly, 44*(5), 635–674.

Sanders, M., Galindo, C., & Allen, K. M. (2021). Professional capital and responses to student diversity: A qualitative exploration of the role of teachers in full-service community schools. *Urban Education, 56*(10), 1782–1814.

Satir, V., Gomori, M., Gerber, J., & Banman, J. (2006). *The Satir model: Family therapy and beyond*. Science and Behavior Books.

Scherff, L. (2018). Distinguishing professional learning from professional development. *Regional Educational Laboratory Pacific*. https://ies.ed.gov/ncee/edlabs/regions/pacific/blogs/blog2_DistinguishingProfLearning.asp

Senge, P. M. (1990). *The fifth discipline: The art and practice of the learning organization*. Currency/Doubleday.

Sims, R. L., & Penny, G. R. (2015). Examination of a failed professional learning community. *Journal of Education and Training Studies, 3*(1), 39–45.

Snow, J. L., Martin, S. D., & Dismuke, S. (2015). "We do more than discuss good ideas": A close look at the development of professional capital in an elementary education liaison group. *Teacher Education Quarterly, 42*(2), 43–63.

The World Cafe. (n.d). *World cafe method*. https://theworldcafe.com/key-concepts-resources/world-cafe-method/

Timperley, H. (2011). *Revitalizing the power of professional learning*. McGraw-Hill.

TNTP. (2013). *Reimagine teaching: New teacher onboarding and cultivation*. https://tntp.org/assets/covid-19-toolkit-resources/Virtual_Onboarding_and_Cultivation_Guide_TNTP.pdf

TNTP. (2022). *Unlocking acceleration: How below grade-level work is holding students back in literacy*. Author. https://tntp.org/assets/documents/Unlocking_Acceleration_8.16.22.pdf

U.S. Department of Education, Office of Educational Technology. (2014). *Professional learning strategies self-assessment tool*. https://tech.ed.gov/wp-content/uploads/2014/11/Section-3-Strategies-Self-Assessment-FINAL.pdf

Vangrieken, K., Dochy, F., Raes, E., & Kyndt, E. (2015). Teacher collaboration: A systematic review. *Educational Research Review, 15*, 17–40.

Vescio, V., Ross, D., & Adams, A. (2008). A review of research on the impact of professional learning communities on teaching practice and student learning. *Teaching and Teacher Education, 24*, 80–91.

Visible Learning Meta[X]. (2021). https://www.visiblelearningmetax.com

Wenger, E., McDermott, R., & Snyder, W. M. (2002). *A guide to managing knowledge: Cultivating communities of practice*. Harvard Business.

INDEX

Academic goals of new teachers, 127

Accountability, 23

Achievement versus progress, 134 (figure)

Action planning, 105, 106–107 (figure), 109–110

Activation, 18–19, 111

Activators

    determining core, 112–114, 113 (figure)

    essential question, 6, 111–112

    having support structures in place for core, 116–117, 117 (figure)

    self-assessment, 118–119

    support school's or district's professional learning, 115, 116 (figure)

Alignment of PLC+ with teachers

    essential question, 6, 65–66

    goals of professional learning and, 74

    learning walks and, 69–71

    microteaching and, 72–73, 72 (figure)

    preserving the learning in a PLC and, 66–67, 67 (figure)

    self-assessment, 75–76

    types of professional learning and, 68–69, 68 (figure)

American Association for Educational Research, 9

Amplifier, the, 85

Assessments

    bias in, 29, 30–31 (figure)

    formative, 13

Attitude, employee, 50 (figure)

Bandura, A., 81

Barriers to learning, 20

Baseline for measurement, 23

Biases, assessment, 29, 30–31 (figure)

Brown, 145

Capacity-building learning walks, 70–71

Capital, 2–3, 163

Change, spreading of, 140–143, 141 (figure)

Clarity, 23, 112–114, 113 (figure)

Climate, school, 42, 42 (figure)

Coaching, 105

Collaboration, 15, 27

    decay and, 16–17

    new teachers and, 125–126

Collaborative Communications Group, 155, 158, 161

Collective teacher efficacy (CTE), 34, 80–82

Common challenges, 158

    checklist of, 59–60, 59 (figure)

    protocol for, 61, 61–62 (figure)

    self-assessment, 63

Communication, 23

    developing effective strategies for, 155–162, 157 (figure), 160 (figure)

    essential question, 6, 153–154

    self-assessment, 163

    Step 1: Who do you want to reach?, 156

    Step 2: What do you want to achieve?, 156, 157 (figure)

    Step 3: What do you want to say?, 158–159, 160 (figure)

    Step 4: How will you send your message?, 161–162

Competence, 77, 79, 112–114, 113 (figure)

Confidence, 112–114, 113 (figure)

Confirmation bias, 30 (figure)

Consciousness, 112–114, 113 (figure)

Core activators. See Activators

Core statement, 158, 160 (figure)

Course-alike teams, 11

Creativity, employee, 50 (figure)

Credibility. See Teacher credibility and collective teacher efficacy

Cross-cutting values, 18–20, 18 (figure)

Data, 101–104

    team trend, 104–108, 106–107 (figure)

Decay, 16–17

Decisional capital, 2–3, 163

Decision making, 98–101, 100 (figure)

Diffusion, 141, 143

Digital message boards, 161
Direction, employee, 50 (figure)
Dissemination, 141–142, 143, 149,
     150 (figure)
DuFour, R., 9
Dynamism, 77, 78, 79

Eaker, R. E., 9
Effectiveness of PLC+
     common formative assessments
          not the only way to talk about
          evidence and, 13
     course-alike teams only one way to
          structure learning communities
          and, 11
     essential question, 6, 9
     Response to Intervention (RTI)/
          Multi-Tiered Systems of Support
          (MTSS) and, 12
     self-assessment, 14
     SMART goals not necessary for PLC
          success and, 10
Empowerment, 23
Equity, 18, 19–20
Expectations, 18, 22–23, 22 (figure)
     of new teachers, 125
Experience, 89

Family and community stakeholders,
     informing of, 161
Feedback, 105
Fifth Discipline, The, 9
Formation of PLC+ teams
     essential question, 6, 87–88
     learning from other organizations
          and, 94
     self-assessment, 95
     types of PLC team configurations and,
          89–93, 90 (figure)
Formative assessments, 13
Fullan, M., 2

Gallery walks, 144–145, 148 (figure)
Ghost walks, 70
Goals. See Team goals, PLC+
Greenhalgh, T., 140
Guiding questions, 18–20, 18 (figure)

Handford, V., 153–154
Hargreaves, A., 2
Hattie, J., 3, 19, 132
Hord, S. M., 9, 15, 42, 139

How do we move learning forward?,
     32, 36–37
Human capital, 2, 163

Ideal state, 20, 21 (figure), 24–25
Identification of trends and development
     of plans to support educators
     essential question, 6, 97–98
     exploring data for, 101–104
     leveled decision making and,
          98–101, 100 (figure)
     self-assessment, 109–110
     team trend data and, 104–108,
          106–107 (figure)
Illusion of knowledge, 30 (figure)
Immediacy, 77, 78, 79
Impact of PLC+ teams
     communication of
          (See Communication)
     confidence that the collective can
          lead to a better interpretation and
          direction and, 135–137
     determining, 132
     essential question, 6, 131
     processes that support noticing and,
          132–135, 134 (figure)
     self-assessment, 138
Implementation, 142, 143, 149, 150 (figure)
Independent contractor, the, 85
Independent learning, 90 (figure)
Individual and collective efficacy, 18
Innovations across schoolwide PLC+
     communication of, 156, 157 (figure)
     from dissemination to implementation,
          149, 150 (figure)
     essential question, 6, 139–140
     formal structures to spread,
          144–147, 146 (figure), 148 (figure)
     how change is spread and,
          140–143, 141 (figure)
     self-assessment, 151
Institute for Organization Management, 23
Instructional leadership. See also Teachers
     beliefs about employees and,
          49, 50 (figure)
     collaboration by, 15, 16–17, 27
     identification of trends and
          development of plans to support
          educators (See Identification of
          trends and development of plans
          to support educators)
     role in PLC+, 1–2

shared and supportive, 41
   as student-centered, 3
   tight-loose (*See* Tight-loose-tight
      model)
   Visible Learning and, 3–4
Intentional collective learning, 41

Key messages, 158, 160 (figure)
Knowles, M. S., 65
Kruse, S., 42

Leana, C., 2
Learning walks, 69–71
Leithwood, K., 153–154
Leveled decision making,
   98–101, 100 (figure)
Loner, the, 85

Maslow, A., 49, 124
Mastery experiences, 81
McGregor, D., 49
Mental orientation, 89
Mentorship, 89
Microteaching, 72–73, 72 (figure)
Motivation, 50 (figure), 89
Multi-Tiered Systems of
   Support (MTSS), 12
Myers, C. B., 9
Myers, L. K., 9

New teachers
   academic goals and, 127
   basic needs of, 124
   community and, 125–126
   essential question, 6, 121–122
   expectations of, 125
   hierarchy of needs for, 123, 123 (figure)
   professional growth of, 127, 128 (figure)
   self-assessment, 129
Next generation PLC+
   decay and, 16–17
   essential question, 6, 15
   guiding questions and cross-cutting
      values and, 18–20
   ideal state and, 20, 21 (figure),
      24–25
   self-assessment, 24–25
   setting expectations to frame the work
      ahead and, 22–23, 22 (figure)
Noticing, 132–135, 134 (figure)

Optimism bias, 30 (figure)

Peer support in PLCs, 41
Pessimism bias, 30 (figure)
Plato, 20
PLC+ (professional learning communities)
   activators (*See* Activators)
   addressing inequity, 18, 19–20
   alignment with teachers (*See*
      Alignment of PLC+ with teachers)
   characteristics of, 6, 39, 40–41 (figure),
      44–46
   effectiveness of (*See* Effectiveness
      of PLC+)
   formation of (*See* Formation
      of PLC+ teams)
   framework of, 5 (figure),
      18 (figure)
   guiding questions and cross-cutting
      values in, 18–20
   impact of (*See* Impact of PLC+ teams)
   innovations across schoolwide
      (*See* Innovations across
      schoolwide PLC+)
   instructional leader's role in, 1–2
   key ideas and essential
      questions in, 6
   major outcomes and commitment
      to, 163
   next generation (*See* Next
      generation PLC+)
   origins of, 9
   professional capital of schools and,
      2–3
   purpose and organization of playbook
      for, 4–7, 5 (figure)
   school climate and, 42
   strong relationship between teacher
      credibility and collective teacher
      efficacy and (*See* Teacher
      credibility and collective teacher
      efficacy)
   success criteria for, 22–23,
      22 (figure)
   team goals (*See* Team goals, PLC+)
   tight-loose-tight model (*See*
      Tight-loose-tight model)
   Visible Learning and, 3–4, 19
Presentations, effective,
   68–69, 68 (figure)
Principal meetings, 162
Professional capital, 2–3
Professional development,
   66–67, 67 (figure)

Professional learning
 differentiated from professional
  development, 66–67, 67 (figure)
 ensuring activators can support
  school's or district's, 115, 116 (figure)
 goals of, 74
 learning walks and, 69–71
 microteaching and, 72–73, 72 (figure)
 for new teachers, 127, 128 (figure)
 types of, 68–69, 68 (figure)
Professional learning communities.
 See PLC+ (professional learning
 communities)
Professional Learning Communities at
 Work, 9
"Professional Learning Communities:
 Communities of Continuous Inquiry
 and Improvement," 9

Quality questions for PLC+
 essential question, 6, 27
 how do we move learning forward?,
  32, 36–37
 how to use, 35
 self-assessment, 36–38
 what did we learn today?, 33, 37
 where are we going?, 28, 36
 where are we now?, 29–31,
  30–31 (figure), 36
 who benefited and who did not
  benefit?, 34, 37
Quiet doers, 44

Readiness to learn, 89
Reference points, 23
Regulation of affective states, 81, 82
Reliance on partial information, 30 (figure)
Response to Intervention (RTI), 12
Responsibility, employee, 50 (figure)
Robinson, V., 3, 95

School and district leaders, informing of,
 161–162
School climate, 42, 42 (figure)
Self-assessment
 activators, 118–119
 common challenges, 63
 communication strategies, 163
 formation of PLC+ teams, 95
 ideal state, 24–25
 impact of PLC+ teams, 138

 innovations across schoolwide
  PLC+, 151
 new teachers, 129
 professional learning, 75–76
 quality questions, 36–38
 sphere of concern, sphere
  of influence, 14
 teacher credibility and efficacy, 85
 team trends, 109–110
 tight-loose-tight model, 53
Self-direction, 89, 90 (figure)
Senge, P., 9
Senior district leadership, 162
Shared and supportive leadership, 41
Shared values and vision of PLCs, 40
SMART goals, 10, 55
Social capital, 2, 163
Social media outlets, 161
Social persuasion, 81, 82
Specific enabling conditions that allow
 professional learning communities to
 thrive key idea
 essential question, 6, 39,
  40–41 (figure)
 school climate fostering,
  42, 42 (figure)
 what went wrong and what went right
  in, 42–46
Sphere of concern, 14
Sphere of influence, 14
Status quo bias, 30 (figure)
Structural conditions of PLCs, 40
Student-centered leadership, 3
Success criteria, 22–23,
 22 (figure)
Supporting points, 159, 160 (figure)
Supportive relational
 conditions of PLCs, 40
System-level learning walks, 162

Talker, the, 85
Teacher credibility and collective teacher
 efficacy
 as activator, 112–114, 113 (figure)
 collective teacher efficacy (CTE)
  and, 34, 80–82
 competence and, 77, 79
 dynamism and, 77, 79
 essential question, 6, 77
 four aspects of, 77–80
 immediacy and, 77, 79

interplay between, 83–84,
83–84 (figure)
self-assessment, 85
trustworthiness and, 77, 79
Teachers. *See also* Instructional
leadership
collaboration by, 15, 16–17, 27
four types of, 84 (figure), 85
new (*See* New teachers)
role in PLC+, 1–2
Team goals, PLC+
common challenge protocol and, 61,
61–62 (figure)
essential question, 6, 55–58,
56 (figure)
quality common challenges checklist
and, 59–60, 59 (figure)
self-assessment, 63
SMART, 10, 55
Team trend data, 104–108,
106–107 (figure)
Theory X, 49, 50 (figure)
Theory Y, 49, 50 (figure)

Tight-loose-tight model
beliefs about employees and,
49, 50 (figure)
characteristics of, 51–52, 51 (figure)
essential question, 6, 47–48,
48 (figure)
self-assessment, 53
Transformation, 89
Trustworthiness, 77, 79

U.S. Chamber of Commerce, 23

Vicarious learning, 81, 82
Visible Learning, 3–4, 19, 80

What did we learn today?, 33, 37
Where are we going?, 28, 36
Where are we now?, 29–31,
30–31 (figure), 36
Who benefited and who did not benefit?,
34, 37
World Cafe method, 145–147, 146 (figure),
148 (figure)

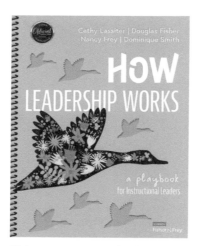
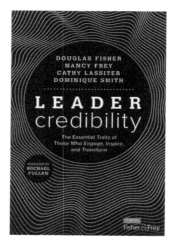

Put your learning into practice

When you're ready to take your learning deeper, begin your journey with our PD services. Our personalized professional learning workshops are designed for schools or districts who want to engage in high-quality PD with a certified consultant, measure their progress, and evaluate their impact on student learning.

CORWIN PLC+

Empower teacher teams to build collective agency and remove learning barriers

It's not enough to just build teacher agency, we must also focus on the power of the collective. Empowering your PLCs is a step toward becoming better equipped educators with greater credibility to foster successful learners.

Get started at corwin.com/plc

CORWIN Teacher Clarity

Students learn more when expectations are clear

As both a method and a mindset, Teacher Clarity allows the classroom to transform into a place where teaching is made clear. Learn how to explicitly communicate to students what they will be learning on a given day, why they're learning it, and how to know if they were successful.

Get started at corwin.com/teacherclarity

CORWIN Visible Learning+®

Translate the science of how we learn into practices for the classroom

Discover how learning works and how this translates into potential for enhancing and accelerating learning. Learn how to develop a shared language of learning and implement the science of learning in schools and classrooms.

Get started at corwin.com/visiblelearning

Experience the Corwin Difference. Learn more at corwin.com/the-corwin-difference

A Sage Company

CORWIN HAS ONE MISSION: to enhance education through intentional professional learning.

We build long-term relationships with our authors, educators, clients, and associations who partner with us to develop and continuously improve the best evidence-based practices that establish and support lifelong learning.